COURSE
MANAGEMENT

Loving Golf…Mastering Life!

KYLE RODGERS

COURSE
MANAGEMENT

TABLE OF CONTENTS

INTRODUCTION

Golf is deceptively simple and endlessly complicated; it satisfies the soul and frustrates the intellect. It is at the same time rewarding and maddening—and it is without a doubt the greatest game mankind has ever invented.
–Arnold Palmer

Golf is a mental game. It can make you crazy. To shoot low rounds, it's necessary to figure out the course. You need to know what to do with your swing, how to blast out of the traps, and how to manage the green. The Golden Bear, Jack Nicklaus, said profoundly, "A big part of managing a golf course is managing your swing on the course. A lot of guys can go out and hit a golf ball, but have no idea how to manage what they do with the ball." Course management is essential. And the same applies to your life.

Golf and life—to *Master* both, excuse the pun, is a challenging task. By observing parallels between the game of golf and the game of life, I hope to equip you with simple yet profound concepts that can enable you to not only manage your life for more fulfillment, but also experience amazing success in the process. That is the "why" of this book. The comparisons I draw between golf and life/leadership, I admit, are obvious; I don't apologize for that. Tethering together powerful words can create indelible principles to alter the round we call life.

It really doesn't matter what hole you are on or whether you have experienced success or failure on life's front nine.

This book can help you excel. Chi Chi Rodriguez said; "Golf is a thinking man's game. You can have all the shots in the bag, but if you don't know what to do with them, you got troubles."

So, if you understand that there is more to be done, more to be accomplished, more significance to be experienced, then join me. Humility will be essential. Drive will be a must. But I promise you can change your game.

Let's go. See you on the links.

PRE-ROUND: PREPARE

To give yourself the best possible chance of playing to your potential, you must prepare for every eventuality. That means practice.
—Seve Ballesteros

A s you consider a day of golf, you understand that preparation is essential. There are a lot of little details to manage. You prepare your sticks and make sure you have the right golf balls. You check to make sure you have your favorite gloves and that the cart is charged. You try and arrive early for your round because a late arrival shortens your warm up. You are even aware that a lack of preparation can be disrespectful to others that may be depending on you in some way. In short, you try to think of everything. When you forget to prepare, or are too lazy to, it shows in your game. It's the same in our daily life. How often do we "ho hum" the mindless details of life and find ourselves unprepared, running around with no semblance of order?

A lack of preparation results in poor time management. Do you have a friend or family member that you falsify times to? You tell them an event starts thirty minutes before it actually does because you know they will be late. Are you that person? You know who I'm talking about . . . Not being prepared wreaks havoc on your time and everyone else's. Most people have a pretty good idea where they will be going on a day-to-day basis. Taking a little time to get organized will make your entire day go much smoother.

Remember, punctuality is a measure of respect for your time as well as others' time. "To be early is to be on time. To be on time is to be late. To be late is unacceptable."

A major example of the cost of being ill-prepared is the significant amount of productivity that is lost because of misplaced items and our quest to find them. According to US News and World Report, the average American will spend one year of their life looking for lost or misplaced items.[1] If gaining a year of your life back is not reason enough to step up your preparation game, I don't know what is. Now, I admit that I have particularly strong feelings about this specific example because it happens to be one of my biggest pet peeves. Have you ever seen a crazy-eyed dog that will not leave a tree because it knows the squirrel is in it? That's me. If I have misplaced something, I literally cannot think about nor do anything else until I find what is lost. My wife, on the other hand, lives by the "all things can be replaced" motto.

Preparation is important in every area of our lives, but it is not necessarily easy. It forces you to think and organize. It requires focusing on the details. Often, it seems like extra work and time. But I'd be willing to wager that if you looked back on your life and studied the occasions that you would consider the outcome mediocre or even an all-out failure, lack of preparation can be attributed. Let's take the concept one step further. There will be times when you may experience difficulty because you depended on someone who was ill-prepared. This is a big deal, my friends. Our lives, successes, and failures coexist. Your preparation or lack thereof can and will affect others. I think it is safe to say that these practices may not come naturally for everyone. But the good news is: preparation can be learned by practicing little disciplines until they become habits.

Preparation creates power and brings you one step closer to winning. Prepared people lead an optimistic, excited existence and live life to its fullest. Preparation and intentional planning allows you to safely navigate life and its challenges. It helps you leave a legacy. People will learn to depend on you. Preparation provides peace, health and well-being. If you recommit to or shore up the details of your life, you can help those dear to you. It is important to leave life better for others by bettering yourself. Especially as we move in to more mature years in our lives, covering the bases for our families and friends is essential. At whatever juncture in life there is solid value in Pre-Round preparation.

Seneca, a first century Roman philosopher said, "Luck is what happens when preparation meets opportunity." Don't miss out on the best life has to offer you because of lack of preparation or intentional planning. Preparation allows you to meet your full potential.

TAKEAWAY PRINCIPLES ON PREPARATION:

1.   If you looked back on your life and studied the occasions that you would consider the outcome mediocre or even an all-out failure, lack of preparation can be attributed.

2.   Preparation practices may not come naturally for everyone. But the good news is, it can be learned by practicing little disciplines until they become habits.

3.   Preparation creates power and brings you one step closer to winning.

Simple Steps:

1.   Consider starting a morning routine. Create a list of things that you do every day to maximize your time and help you prepare for your day.

2.   Make it a habit to look over your calendar every week to see what you have coming in advance.

3.   Pick one area of your life that you seem to struggle with being unprepared for. Make a plan for how to master that area. It could be family birthdays, inventories at work, or your gym workouts. Pick one. Make a plan. Execute. Then pick another.

RECOMMENDED READING:

- *Intentional Living by John Maxwell*
- *Power of Habit by Charles Duhigg*

WELL THAT'S INTERESTING . . .

Call it preparation, call it superstition. But here are a few claimed practices of some of the world's most famous golfers.[2]

- Jack Nicklaus will never play a round of golf without three coins in his pocket—and it must be exactly three, no more, no less. The denominations don't matter. Just as long as three coins are jingling in his pocket, he can step out to the first tee.

- Ben Crenshaw has been known to only bring golf balls with numbers one through four on them because he claims that anything higher may result in scores that equal the same.
- Zach Johnson does not play a round without a very special ball marker that his wife Kim made for him. The custom ball marker holds biblical phrases and verses.
- Davis Love III only uses white tees and marks his balls on the green with only 1965 or 1966 pennies—any coin minted after that might bring him bad luck.
- Fred Funk flips a coin before marking his ball on the green. If the coin lands on tails, then he marks his ball with the tail facing up in a normal fashion. If it comes up heads, he'll turn the coin to make sure the head is facing the hole.

NOTES

HOLE #1: INTEGRITY

THE FOUNDATION OF YOUR GAME

To find a man's true character, play golf with him.
–P. G. Wodehouse

Golf is the only game where you call a foul on yourself.
–Joe Torre

O ne of my favorite moments as a golf fan are the first hole introductions. There are always other interested fans that line the tee box and talk in excited hushed tones among themselves. I love to see the participants, hear where they are from, and honor them with a resounding "golf clap." I always observe their body language; you can almost see their anticipation—nerves on full display.

The first hole of any golf match is critical. You know, your approach, that first swing. You have to deal with the nerves. It is almost impossible not to feel the eyes focused only on you and what you're about to do. You feel the tightness. Possibly lacking course familiarity or acclimation to the environment, you're not in the groove yet. People often remember how we start, which is why first impressions are so important and intimidating.

Integrity is your foundation. It's hole #1 for life. Here's the deal though, I want to talk about real integrity, not just what you outwardly display. You might possess the ability to manipulate people's perceptions of you while never possessing inner integrity. Integrity is doing the right thing, whether anyone sees it or not. It's being true to your beliefs, to the point that your external actions match your internal beliefs. It's your relationship with you. Why not love yourself and what you believe so much that you dedicate a full effort into being the same inwardly as what is evidenced outwardly. Integrity, true integrity, will require you to be brutally honest with yourself first and foremost. This is what I call *holistic integrity*; it's harmony between what you believe, what you say, and what you do. No contradictions. Like in golf, where players have total respect for every facet of the game, and it shows in the way they practice when no one is looking and the way they play when there is an audience. Lou Holtz, famed football coach and golf enthusiast said, "In golf, the player, coach, and official are all rolled into one and they overlap completely. Golf is the best microcosm of life, or at least the way life should be." Do you see the implication here? They overlap completely. In life, you have to have the discipline to be all three in one: player, coach, and official. You enjoy being the participant, you have to coach yourself, and you must enforce the rules of the game. That's holistic integrity.

So how do you become a person of integrity? The first step is a desire for winning the war of right and wrong on a daily basis. One shot at a time. One swing, then another; every little victory adds up. Each win moves you to greater confidence. It's like the effect of a consistent workout on your body. You get stronger and more resilient with each win. You will also learn that although failure is inevitable, it too will strengthen your integrity (we will go into depth about the education of failure on a later hole).

Integrity, like the first hole of any golf match, is difficult. And as does the first hole, integrity charts the course for your life. What you do incrementally, or on a daily basis becomes your life's message. It's who you are. Your disposition, the way you respond, the way you treat others, the vibes you give off, all determine your level of integrity. Integrity or the lack thereof is the offspring of each and every decision you make. The direction you go in life is a result of those decisions—the simple and the complex. So, take time to think them through.

It's so critical in life to start anything well. I preach passionately to adolescents to take their formative years very seriously. The habits formed when you are young are the habits you will take with you all of your life. The sometimes negative, self-absorbed habits formed as a child can haunt you as an adult. And, unfortunately, people struggle their whole lives with tendencies formed early. That is why parents and grandparents should take very seriously the roles they play in an adolescent's view on life and decision making. Simply put, like in an excursion to the links, if you start well you will always have an advantage.

Side note: Please don't allow early life mistakes to discourage you. It is never too late to create new habits and build an even stronger foundation. Sometimes to be old and wise requires you to be young and stupid.

Integrity is ultimately the brand you choose for your life. Your brand of integrity is your public proclamation of who you are, what you believe, and how you have decided to invest your life. What if you don't like your current brand? Can you change? The answer to that is an emphatic YES! It will take time. It will require commitment and buckets of humility. Most people aren't truly willing to do what it takes for real change in character and integrity. You will have to be brutally honest with yourself. To connect with other people will require you connecting with yourself. Remember you can fool others, but you can't fool yourself.

Your credibility is invaluable. Never tamper with your credibility; take it seriously. Life is all about relationships. Your future will require connection with people who will evaluate you based on your credibility. And integrity is getting harder to find in this world. So, protect it like the valuable commodity it is.

What I am propagating here may seem like a lonely road. It's a little like standing by yourself in the middle of the golf course, attempting desperately to hit a good shot. To be totally engaged in a life of integrity may cost you. The energy invested is worth it, so do whatever it takes. Success on hole #1 is critical. The road to integrity is narrow, but there is room for you.

Takeaway Principles on Integrity:

1.   Integrity is ultimately the brand you choose for your life. Your brand of integrity is your public proclamation of who you are, what you believe, and how you have decided to invest your life.

2.   Why not love yourself and what you believe so much that you dedicate a full effort, into being the same inwardly as what is evidenced outwardly.

3.   Honesty is more important than victory, and success without integrity is failure.

SIMPLE STEPS:

1.   Keep your word. Do what you say you are going to do. If you are unsure whether you can make a commitment, then don't say "yes." Get good at saying "no" while you learn your capacity.

2.   Choose your friends wisely. I agree with Franklin Roosevelt when he said, "Show me your friends, I'll show you your future." Think carefully about the people you associate with. Who do you need to spend less time with? On the flip side, who do you know that exemplifies integrity? Make a point to spend more time with them.

3.   Take 100 percent responsibility. All the time. Don't blame the government, your coworker, or your wife.

4.   Guard your heart and mind—be careful of what you are feeding them. Your heart and mind are the primary agents responsible for your decisions and every decision, no matter how small, builds or tears down your integrity.

RECOMMENDED READING:

- *Integrity: The Courage to Meet the Demands of Reality by Dr. Henry Cloud*
- *Return on Integrity: The New Definition of ROI and Why Leaders Need to Know It by John G. Blumberg*

Well That's Interesting . . .

Robert "Bobby" Jones may not be a household name, but he is considered to be one of history's greatest golfers. He won thirteen majors before he retired at the ripe old age of twenty-eight. He is also the only person in the history of golf to win the Grand Slam—all four major championships in the same calendar year. Even Tiger hasn't done that. But what many would consider his greatest achievement might be his self-imposed one-stroke penalty that cost him the 1925 US Open.

In June of 1925, Jones was in a *second* eighteen-hole playoff against Willie McFarlane for the US Open Championship. On the eleventh hole, Jones hit his shot a little to the right, and found the rough. It wasn't an impossible shot, but there was a lot of grass and twigs around his ball. After choosing his club, he addressed the ball, and, according to Jones, it moved a just a bit.

Now, in golf if the ball moves in any way, *even unintentionally,* it's a one-shot penalty. No one saw the ball move except him—not his playing partner, not even his caddie. But Jones called the one-shot penalty on himself anyway. It cost him the game.

The tournament official asked, "Do you believe you touched the ball?" To which Bobby responded, "I know that I did." When the official tried to praise him for his actions, Jones said, "You may as well praise a man for not robbing a bank.

NOTES

NOTES

HOLE #2: POTENTIAL

APPRECIATE THE CLUBS YOU WERE GIVEN

Everyone can see my swing is homegrown. That means everyone has a chance to do it.
—Bubba Watson

Have you ever considered the "best you"? If we truly believe God created us and He makes no mistakes, then finding the greatness within is worth pursuing. When one discovers their true design and recognizes that greatness, it's much easier to believe you can accomplish great things. I can't personally pull out a person's infinite potential. What I can give is encouragement and hopefully a little motivation to help you find it. Life is all about becoming the best version of yourself. Now go after it.

Circumstances and environment can certainly help mold us, but we are all pre-wired with a certain temperament. You were born with certain natural talents and gifts. Your heart is passionate about some things more than others. You may change in life as you grow but you will always be you. John Ortberg puts it this way in *The Me I Want to Be*, "An acorn can grow into an oak tree, but it cannot become a rose bush." Quit worrying about what you are not and start being thankful for what you are—that's how you grow.

Here's the challenge: take an honest look at yourself. I mean really do some internal evaluation. Take some time to think about your strengths and preferences. List them if you feel compelled. If you want to go deeper, you could look at taking a test like the Myers Briggs to get a better insight into your wiring and personality. You have been gifted with some pretty fine equipment that was custom designed specifically for you. Take stock of it. And quit worrying about what clubs everybody else is using.

I have always been a bit fascinated by hoarders. The fact that they cannot part with anything, I find unhealthy but interesting. My wife likes to give me a hard time and say I have hoarder tendencies. So maybe I did dig a candle back out of the trash after she threw it away. I just firmly believe everything has value and has been created for a reason. Everything wants to be used as it was designed. It functions better. I know you can think of a time when you used something for a purpose it totally was not created for. A shoe as a hammer? A bucket as a step stool? A cat as a door stop? Kidding. But you get the point. They may have served a purpose but not very well. Same goes with us. We will best excel when we utilize our strengths and work as we were designed to.

Don't be discouraged with the "now" of your situation. Pick one small thing you can work on and start there. Use what you have to continue to progress in self-betterment—this is how you'll reach your full potential. Don't use someone else's standard; this isn't a comparison game. This is about knowing yourself. Do your best right now to get through whatever trap you may be in. And then come out ready to keep swinging. Be warned, however, when you make the cognitive choice to better your life by pursuing your vision, some will not like it. Being stagnant in your life has enabled others to stay stagnant too. Your choice to change will bring attention to their choice to do nothing. Don't judge them too harshly, you too have been in their position. Don't allow their attitude to hold you back. Be courageous and move on.

Maybe you once had dreams but now they have been relegated to the back shelf for so long that you can't recall what they were. Let's reclaim them. Let's decide what we want to be when we grow up again. When I was young, I would often wonder how tall I would be, how fast I would run, or how high I would be able to jump. My keen interest in sports was always the filter. How could I take my gifting and become the best? What's sad is, at some point, I stopped wondering. I can't remember when.

At what point in life do we lose that wonderment? Where does the awe and the marveling go? Why grow up? Why grow old? Whatever we were doing that brought wonder and energy, vitality and passion, let's bring it back. Passion is what moves men and women to action. Why did you stop _____? You fill in the blank. You were at one time jazzed about certain areas in your life. What made you stop? The good thing is, you can choose to go after them again. Even if circumstances don't seem ideal, go anyway.

Be careful with the language of "later" or "someday." Monday through Sunday is on every calendar, but you never see Someday. Be vigilant as you plan and prepare for the "some-time soon" of your life. It's true and noble to be responsible. The kids may need to get a little older or one may need to pay off a bill or two. I get it. The point is: proceed! Prepare a strategy. Discipline yourself to arrange details that will move you in the direction you have wanted to go. Every day has value and we should never waste one, so start now.

Mr. Watson finished his quote with: "I just want to be me and play golf. I'm just Bubba." What sage words. Go be you.

TAKEAWAY PRINCIPLES ON POTENTIAL:

1. Each one of us was born with specific inherencies that make us uniquely us.

2. Quit worrying about what you are not and start being thankful for what you are. That's how you grow.

3. We will best excel when we utilize our strengths and work as we were designed to.

4. Prepare a strategy. Discipline yourself to arrange details that will move you in the direction you have wanted to go. Every day has value, and we should never waste a day, so start now.

SIMPLE STEPS:

1. Make a list of what you believe are some of your personal strengths. Ask one or two people close to you to give you input as well.

2. Take a strength finding test like the Myers Briggs or the Enneagram to see what's underneath the cape and get to know more about your super powers.

3. Set five reasonable new goals. Write them down. Numerous studies have found you become at least 40 percent more likely to achieve your goals and dreams, simply by writing them down on a regular basis. Then set five unreasonable goals. Be as far-fetched as you can. (Ex: President of _____ or the worlds fittest _____ year old.) Don't discount this exercise. Many will reach these goals.

4. Call someone you consider to be an overcomer. Invite them to coffee. Ask them to tell you their story.

RECOMMENDED READING:

- *The Road Back to You: An Enneagram Journey to Self-Discovery by* <u>Ian Morgan Cron</u> *and* <u>Suzanne Stabile</u>
- *The Mind Styles Model: Theory, Principles and Practice by Anthony F. Gregorc*
- *Do Over: Rescue Monday, Reinvent Your Work, and Never Get Stuck by Jon Acuff*

WELL THAT'S INTERESTING. . .

You have been gifted with some pretty fine equipment that was custom designed specifically for you. Take stock of it. Speaking of taking stock in your equipment, here are two of the most famous clubs in history. [1]

<u>Calamity Jane</u>

"It was rusty and sort of beat up and no doubt had several owners before it every got to me," said Bobby Jones of his "cracked-hickory-shafted" putter that he used to win his first three majors. The original Calamity Jane, which is housed today at Augusta National, gave way to a successor, Calamity Jane II, and while that club wasn't much to look at either, it worked just fine for Jones, who won ten more major titles with CJII in his bag.

White Fang

In 1997, at his son Steve's thirty-fourth birthday party, Jack received the most memorable gift of all: a Bulls Eye putter, its face speckled with white paint. A broken pencil was jammed into the butt end of its grip. Nicklaus recognized it right away as the club he'd nicknamed White Fang, the putter he'd used on his way to winning the '67 US Open at Baltusrol.

After the championship, Nicklaus had stored White Fang in a bin in his Florida home; Steve, unaware of the club's significance, had picked it up and loaned it to a friend, who took his time returning it. White Fang now resides where it belongs: at the Jack Nicklaus Museum at Ohio State University.

NOTES

NOTES

HOLE #3: HONOR

RESPECT THE GAME AND THE PLAYERS

The object of golf is not just to win. It is to play like a gentleman and win.
—Phil Mickelson

Golf is an honorable sport. What makes golf an honorable sport is not the rules of the game but the honorable people who have played the game. When you hear the word honor, what comes to mind? For me, what comes to mind is respect for other people. You build a reputation of being a person of honor through your actions towards other people. Are you kind, honest, and attentive? Being a person of honor doesn't mean letting people take advantage of you or losing your competitive edge. You can still seek success while coming by it honestly and respectfully.

We all know the saying "Nice guys finish last." I disagree. Nice guys are winners before the game even begins. There is always a place for nice. It is admirable and attractive. People with polite, unselfish spirits are often confused as weak or pushovers. However, meekness is not weakness; it is power restrained. Kindness and strength go hand-in-hand. In truth, nice people, people of honor, exercise superior self-control. The whole idea of "I just couldn't help myself" is nothing more than obvious weakness. You can help yourself. You should help yourself. Living with honor requires dedication and discipline. A well-mannered person remains committed to the higher calling regardless of the score.

We are all familiar with the Golden Rule, "Do unto others as you would have them do unto you." This is a good basis for not only golf course etiquette but also life. When you live by that rule, you often have a different spirit, a less assuming attitude. You act on purpose and with intention. Honorable people make up their mind after careful deliberation and prepare for every task. They are alert, sharp, and ready to act. They are punctual, knowing how respectful it is to honor someone else's time. Their mood is kind and humble. They are generous, not just financially but as a lifestyle—with their energy and time. A person of honor invests in others. It really is all about respect as it relates to all people and not just a chosen few.

And let us not overlook the power in basic manners. Simple actions speak volumes. Open car doors, house doors, and store doors for others. Stand when others enter a room with a willingness to give up your seat or place to make accommodation. Allow others first place in line—it doesn't hurt to be second. It's not personal condescension, it's all about courtesy and deference. Try to make all around you as comfortable as possible. Pick up stuff, even if it's not yours. Be complimentary and sincerely grateful, never rude or snobbish. "Please" and "thank you" should frequent your lips. You were created with two ears and one mouth to listen twice as much as you speak.

Our world is ever in a free fall of anger and violence. The whole "others first" idea is difficult. It smacks against our natural, human bent. People are always screaming for their own rights. There is a constant cry of, "it's all about me." This lifestyle is hazardous because its end is terminal, deadly. A casual understanding of our world substantiates the point. And the point is . . . We need more honorable people in this world. We also need more golfers. You can be both a winner and a person of honor.

Payne Stewart once said, "In the end it's still a game of golf, and if at the end of the day you can't shake hands with your opponent and still be friends, then you've missed the point." I love the quote and I loved the man. He was a person of honor. It's our turn now.

TAKEAWAY PRINCIPLES ON HONOR:

1.   Honor necessitates respect for others. It's all about respect as it relates to all people and not just a chosen few.

2.   Meekness is not weakness; it is power restrained.

3.   Good manners are always attractive.

SIMPLE STEPS:

1.   How did you react to the honorable person's characteristics? Was there internal push back? Why do you think that is?

2.   Without making a public statement begin an "Open Door" campaign. Open the door for anyone entering or leaving a building at the same time as you. Practice it for a period of time until it becomes second nature.

3.   Do you know someone you would consider a person of honor? Think about the qualities he/she possesses that you admire. Which ones can you start to emulate?

Recommended Reading:

- *How to Win Friends and Influence People by Dale Carnegie*
- *The Gentleman's Book of Etiquette and Manual of Politeness by Cecil B. Hartley*

Well That's Interesting. . .

Samuel L. Jackson on a manners lesson gone awry (December 2005):

"I love to sign autographs for kids but insist they say 'please.' I found myself near the ropes by a large group of kids, all of them waving their programs for me to sign. But I don't hear 'please,' so I figure it's time to enforce the rules. I announce loudly, so the whole gallery can hear, 'What are you supposed to say?' The kids don't answer, they just continue waving the programs. I repeat myself, this time more sternly: 'What's the magic word?' Still no answer. I'm ready to walk away when one of the bigger kids, with a look of total frustration on his face, starts mumbling loudly. Then it hits me: These kids were from a local school for the deaf. Come to find out they're on their annual field trip. As the adults shot me looks, I started signing and didn't stop until our group fell a hole behind."[1]

NOTES

NOTES

HOLE #4: FOCUS

BEWARE OF DISTRACTIONS

*It's such a psychological and mental game, golf, that the smallest wrong thing
at the wrong time can distract you from what you're trying to achieve.*
—*Lee Westwood*

To truly focus on something, we must tune out all distractions. Distractions have the ability to play positive and negative roles in our lives, but for the purpose of this chapter we will be discussing the latter. Distractions and the activity of being distracted can also cover a wide range of subjects, so let's start this hole off by looking at a couple of definitions.

Distraction:

1.   mental distress or derangement: *My boss drives me to distraction.*

2.   that which distracts, divides the attention, or prevents concentration: *The gentleman's flamboyant pants are distracting me.*

3.   that which diverts; amusement; entertainment: *Sports is his major distraction.* [1]

Perhaps the greatest danger on a golf course is distractions. To focus and play well, distractions must be eliminated. For the serious golfer, this is not a suggestion, it's an imperative. In life, the same holds true with goal setting and progress. Nothing steals the punch of dreams like a distraction. However, it may seem almost too simple. Just eliminate the distractions. But don't discount the concepts here on Hole #4 too quickly. Distractions are not always obvious and they can hit from all directions and at all times. Learning to identify and eliminate distractions so you can focus is essential.

I enjoy watching people on the golf course almost as much as I enjoy playing. What's fascinating is the smallest things can invoke an exit from the focus fairway. It can be the pressure you feel, that relaxing drink, the cigar, the cart girl, the bad shot, the phone call . . . you get the idea. In life, distractions are an evil thief; they rob you of success. Significance and success in life mirror a tough golf shot—one little diversion can throw you off. A simple complication can affect the outcome of your dreams. And the purpose for your life is always more valuable than a period of inattentiveness. So, you must stay engaged. Guard your heart, your eyes, your passions, your relationships. Remind yourself daily that you are the custodian of your time on this planet. It involves incredible discipline and concentration, but the payoff is always worth it.

If not carefully monitored, distractions can deflect your values. Distractions are always the easier path, and temptations to take the "short cuts" are alluring. But following the easiest and most appealing path can be damaging. A lifetime of achievement and proficiency can implode with one poor decision as your values come into question. Trust can be compromised within a moment of meandering. When you choose to indulge distractions—and it is a choice—you are investing energy in things outside of God's plan for your life. I often counsel folks who speak of a solitary occasion that brought their house or their business down. Often, I hear these words, "I just wasn't paying attention." Distractions can become controlling without us even realizing it. Look, we all are given a limited amount of time and energy, so be careful with how you use it. Short cuts in life will leave you in a mess. Just like in your golf game, the easy route to the green is often through the hazards. Don't gamble with your values. The real damage comes to your reputation.

Don't allow distractions to disorient your circle of influence. People need to know you are trustworthy and reliable. Especially your family. Would you take a moment and just visualize the faces of those that unequivocally depend on you? They are involved in your journey too. Be careful, determined, conscientious, and sincere with your life's message. Remember life is all about relationships. You may make a choice on your own, but the reaction always includes others.

Sometimes distractions can overtake your agenda. Don't allow this. Be intentional with your time. Poor decisions now can result in a detour or even a significant change of plans later. Filter every daily decision with this question: Will this move me in the right direction? If the honest answer is "no," don't go there. Be courageous, and never let distractions decide your agenda. Make it a priority every day to know what you want to accomplish in a day. Zero in on the steps needed to get to your life's goals. Start today. There are some really helpful online planning and goal setting tools to help you make the most of your time and stay focused. Find one that works for you.

When interviewed by a sports journalist actor, Lucas Black made the following profound statement: "If you're thinking clearly and are content about where your life is—to where you can just think about the present, think about the now—that's what you need to do to hit good golf shots. I know there are a lot of distractions, but when you're thinking clearly, you're more free. You've got to have that freedom on the golf course. It helps you execute that shot at that given moment. And that's really all that golf cares about. It could care less about anything else but that defining moment right at impact."[2] Can you imagine how freeing your life would feel to give up unnecessary distractions? What is holding you back?

Remember, distractions will not always come waltzing in wearing a large scary wolf mask, slinging whiskey, bellowing like a drunken sailor. Distractions are often disguised as good things. But the enemy of "best" is often "good."

Finally, if you have fallen, feel the pain and move on. Learn from it and then let it propel you to a better existence. Listen, the longer you hold on to distractive habits, the heavier the load will get. Find your errors, fix them, and then focus on your future.

TAKEAWAY PRINCIPLES ON FOCUS:

1.   Distractions are not always obvious and can hit from all directions and at all times. Learning how to identify distractions and how to shift your focus is essential.

2.   Significance and success in life mirror a tough golf shot—one little diversion can throw you off.

3.   Sometimes distractions can overtake your agenda. Don't allow this. Be intentional with your time. Poor decisions now can result in a detour or even a significant change of plans later.

SIMPLE STEPS:

1.   What does a negative distraction look like in your life? Make a list. Be aware of what distractions trip you up. Which ones could cost you your reputation?

2.   Think about some distractions that are seemingly not harmful but eat up your time? What is one you could give up?

RECOMMENDED READING:

- *Awaken the Giant Within: How to Take Immediate Control of Your Mental, Emotional, Physical & Financial Destiny! by Anthony Robbins*
- *Eat That Frog!: 21 Ways to Stop Procrastinating and Get More Done in Less Time by Brian Tracy*

WELL THAT'S INTERESTING . . .

When Lee Trevino was asked whether or not too much alcohol might have hurt his chances at the 1968 PGA in San Antonio this was his response:

"That was an accident. That was when Gatorade first came out, and they put a case of it in my room. I was right there by the ninth green. And we were having a party Saturday night, and they were mixing tequila with this stuff, and it was pretty good. And they had all this Gatorade in the refrigerator in a big pot. I went to bed early, because I was in the hunt, only a stroke or two off the lead, and I got up thirsty about 3:00 in the morning.

And I saw this pot of Gatorade in the refrigerator, and I started chug-a-lugging, not knowing there was tequila in it. I woke up blind drunk. It was a scorching-hot day, and I don't know if I ever felt so bad on a golf course. I think I shot 76."[3]

Talk about a distraction!

NOTES

NOTES

HOLE #5: COMPETITION

THE DRIVE TO WIN

If I got a swing, I got a shot!
—Bubba Watson

T he absolute necessity of competition is seen in our great sport. I am a firm believer in healthy competition and the invaluable life lessons you learn when you compete. We need to learn to manage our nerves and control our emotions when things don't go our way in order to have healthy competition. Competition conditions us to take risks. It teaches goal setting and how to bring our best effort. It encourages us to play by the rules. Competition helps us learn at a faster rate and perform at a higher level. I mean who doesn't want that? But the key is "healthy" competition.

Let's examine what I call the "Bitter/Better Principle." In life, if you compete against others as a priority, I would bet you experience bitterness internally. You may find yourself bitter inside particularly when someone beats you. What is sad is that in many cases the opponent may not even really be an opponent. The people God put into your life were not placed there for you to strive against; they were divinely appointed in your life to thrive with! If there's outward competition you may potentially envy others' victories, resulting in a buildup of animosity that hinders you from celebrating their successes. In life, we will come into conflict with people. When we do, we have a choice: we can genuinely root for them to become the significant person they were designed to be or we can agonize over their success. You will always be left with a bitter taste in your mouth if you choose to use others as your competitive fire.

The Better side of this theory is a challenge to compete within yourself. You are more likely to experience satisfaction, greater motivation, personal discipline, and inner confidence if they are not dependent on the performance of someone else. When you compete against yourself, you are forced to see things exactly how they are. You know whether you are investing the right competitive energies to be the best you can be. Which side of the principle do you live on? What was modeled for you? Too many people who endure the comparison game are left feeling worthless and insecure. Your value doesn't decrease based on someone else's increase in value. You are wonderfully made with greatness inside. It's up to you to cultivate it.

I don't care how gifted, intelligent, practiced, or pretty you look on the course—if you can't manage the mental end of the game, you will fail miserably. Bobby Jones agreed when he said, "Competitive golf is played mainly on a five- and one-half inch course, the space between your ears." This is a huge concept.

All great competitors share certain mental attributes that help lead them to wins. Let's examine a few that you can incorporate into your game plan. First, they all have great confidence. How can achieve that? Tell your mind what to think! And no, I am not talking hippy, new-age mantras; I am talking basic neuroscience. You have the ability to "set your mind." At any given moment you can to turn your thoughts in one direction or another.

If we don't pay close attention to our thoughts, then we will be controlled by the content. Tell your mind what you want it to save. Rely on what you know is true rather than assuming the negative of any given situation. It's a never-ending task, I know, but it can change your mental competitive spirit.

Great competitors also live passionately. Without passion you lose energy quickly. Without passion, you live in a rut. Ruts are easy to exist in. They are often comfortable. But they make you lazy and unhealthy. They steal from you. Your mind controls your life, so don't allow a mental thief to have a place there; battle your ruts. Do you want something so badly in life you can almost taste it? Make some plans and make them big! Niccolo Machiavelli the fifteenth century author and philosopher penned these words, "Make no small plans, for they have no power to stir the soul." Big plans will push you. Do you need to make some plans that will invigorate you?

Vulnerability is not usually an attribute you would associate with fierce competition, but successful competitors know when they can let their guard down. It takes a serious amount of mental toughness to be vulnerable. And it may not come easy in the beginning. Do not be afraid to fail or share those failures with people in your inner circle. Failure offers more education than success. Don't be afraid of new ideas or an open-minded approach to concepts. Recognize the need to change and evolve as your goals change and grow. Always be willing to ask for help. Most of all know that you cannot truly grow stronger until you open up to others, acknowledge your weaknesses, and ask for help.

And finally, great competitors practice humility and an attitude of "no regrets." Humility and sportsmanship are such strong principles that we will devote an entire hole to each later on. But for now, let's leave it with: be a humble winner and a humble loser. No one like's an obnoxious, rub-it-in-your-face winner. And the only thing worse is being a cry baby sore loser. So, practice humility. Now let's talk about the importance of adopting a "no regret" policy. Regrets are destructive. And rarely does obsessing over the "I could have done/should have done" moments bring us closer to our goals. So instead ask yourself "Did I do everything I could possibly do to achieve my goal and did I go in with the right attitude"? If the answer is "yes," move on. No looking back. If the answer is "no," take some time to examine what you could have done differently, and learn from it. Then move on. No looking back.

Takeaway Principles on Competition:

1. Healthy competition teaches invaluable life lessons and strengthens character.

2. Your only competition is in the mirror. You are more likely to experience satisfaction, greater motivation, personal discipline, and inner confidence if they are not dependent on the performance of someone else.

3. All great competitors share certain mental attributes that help lead them to wins. A combination of confidence and vulnerability, passion and restraint, pride and humility.

Simple Steps:

1. What propels your competitive fire? Write down a few ways you love to compete.

2.   How do you feel when others experience success?

3.   What are some areas that you desire to win in? Pick one and then make a step-by-step plan to achieve it.

RECOMMENDED READING:

- *Finish Line Thinking: How to Think and Win Like a Champion by Nicky Billou*

WELL THAT'S INTERESTING. . .

During World War II, German aircrafts from Norway would fly on missions to northern England. Often, the soldiers would have to clear their guns due to icy weather conditions. So, as they crossed the coast, they would clear their guns by firing a few rounds at the golf courses.

So, the Golf Course at Richmond Gold Club posted a sign that reads:

** Richmond Golf Club **

* Temporary Rules 1940 *

1. Players are asked to collect bombs and shrapnel to save causing damage to the mowing machines.

2. In competitions, during gunfire players may take cover without incurring a penalty for ceasing playing.

3. The positions of known delayed action bombs are marked with red flags.

4. Shrapnel may be moved on the fairway or in the bunkers, without penalty.

5. A ball moved or destroyed by enemy action can be replaced without penalty, provided it's not nearer the hole.

6. A player whose stroke is affected by a bomb exploding may play another ball from the same place. Penalty one stroke.

Even in the midst of World War II, you could not get golfers to give up on competing![1]

NOTES

NOTES

HOLE #6: SPORTSMANSHIP

NOBODY LIKES A SORE LOSER

It's good sportsmanship to not pick up lost golf balls while they are still rolling.
—Mark Twain

Take a moment with me and visualize someone you think of when you hear the phrase "poor sport" (I'll give you ten seconds. Pretend you hear the Jeopardy theme song.). Did someone immediately pop in your head? For me, it's a kid I played ball with when I was younger. If he didn't like the call or the other team scored, he would throw a fit. Chucking his mitt, yelling expletives, etc. The only reason I didn't punch him was because he was on my team.

Now strike up an image of someone you would consider a "good sport." What thoughts come to mind? Ok next question . . . How do you carry yourself on the golf course? What if I asked someone else the same about you? Would their answers mirror your personal evaluation? I challenge you to take inventory. The outcome of any contest is forgotten over time, but the actions of players, coaches, and spectators are indelibly remembered. Friends, if you fail in sportsmanship, what have you won? Unsportsmanlike behavior is more damaging than a shot in the water, a penalty stroke, or even a fifteen-yard penalty. Unsportsmanlike behavior damages your reputation. True sportsmen are in control of their actions and reactions, because they know that their reputation is their greatest asset.

Every sport has unruly participants whose priorities lack sportsmanship. But because of the methodical slower nature of golf, players and spectators that are behaving poorly tend to stand out like a cowboy in China. Foul language reverberates; all eyes are on you as frivolously waste money with the throwing or breaking of your equipment; every movement and aspect your body language is broadcast.

So, what is sportsmanship and how can we benefit from it in our lives? My personal definition would be this: A good sportsman has the ability to compete passionately without sacrificing his/her integrity. They are fair and honorable to everyone and value people more than their pursuits. They understand that the best part of the game is the opportunity to play. Ralph Waldo Emerson said, "Win as if you were used to it, lose as if you enjoyed it for a change." Again, create a standard that is anything but standard.

I was taught early in life the difference between reaction and response. If you are controlled by your reactions, life can be even more challenging than it needs to be. But if your priorities are set and you are living a disciplined life you will be prepared with the proper response for any situation you may encounter. How often do we excuse our conduct with the "react" defense? You say, "I just couldn't help myself" or "it just happened." What a weak excuse for poor behavior. Responding correctly in the heat of the circumstance isn't easy; it requires disciplined preparation, but after a while thinking before you act becomes second nature. And that's an absolute necessity to be a good sport.

A long time ago I decided to practice giving words of affirmation. I intentionally look for opportunities to say good things to people. Short words of encouragement are helpful for the giver and the receiver; it's a win-win. You win because you gain the victory over your mind by commanding its thoughts, and receivers win as you enrich their lives with simple kindness. And you never know what's going on in a person's life. Your words have the power to change an entire situation. There may be one little corner of someone's heart that is enslaved to insecurity or fear. Positive reinforcement can breathe life into an individual because sincere encouragement has the power to give hope.

I challenge you to periodically look to affirm people as you observe their behaviors. Perhaps you could even set a number as a daily challenge. For instance, I will affirm seven people a day, then observe if their productivity and outlook changes for the better. I believe you will be amazed with the results. As you do this, remember that a self-life is a lost life. If your agenda is only to exalt yourself you will never find contentment or significance. The outcome doesn't matter because true character of sportsmanship is all about how you invest into the lives of people regardless of whether you win or lose. Remember, it's how you play the game that counts.

TAKEAWAY PRINCIPLES ON SPORTSMANSHIP:

1.   Never let a win go to your head or a loss go to your heart.

2.   True sportsmen are in control of their actions and reactions, because they know that their reputation is their greatest asset.

3.   A good sportsman can compete passionately without sacrificing his/her integrity.

SIMPLE STEPS:

1.   Next time you are involved in any type of competition, pay attention to your actions. Take note of what you may need to change. Self-evaluation is a powerful tool.

2.   Practice encouraging others with simple genuine compliments.

RECOMMENDED READING:

- *Sportsmanship: Multidisciplinary Perspectives by Tim Delaney*

WELL THAT'S INTERESTING . . .

If we are going to talk of sportsmanship, I think it is only fitting to revisit what many still call the single greatest show of sportsmanship in golf history: The 1969 Ryder Cup. The entire tournament had been tainted by instances of unsportsmanlike behavior and saucy attitudes on the part of both teams. On the second day, it looked like players were going to go to blows, so captain Sam Snead had to intervene. You know things are bad when the guy called to break up your fight has been described in a 1969 Sports Illustrated article as "a crude, sullen, cantankerous old buzzard [who is] as capable of leadership as Ebenezer Scrooge." Ouch.

On the final hole, Despite the crowd of 8,000 jamming around the green, the silence almost deafening. Both golfers made it to the green in two shots.

Nicklaus' eagle putt was five feet past the hole; Jacklin's was two feet short. Nicklaus sunk his putt for birdie, and then picked up Jacklin's ball marker and conceded the two-foot putt. After three days of tension, acrimony, and near-violence, Nicklaus forced the match, and the tournament, to end in a draw. The first tie in Ryder Cup history.[1]

NOTES

HOLE #7: OPTIMISM

LOOK AT THE BRIGHT SIDE

A bad attitude is worse than a bad swing.
—Payne Stewart

We have all heard countless overused clichés and inspirational quotes about optimism. "See the glass as half full," "When life gives you lemons, make lemonade," "Where there is rain there's a rainbow," and, my personal favorite, "When your horse dies, make glue." Optimism is the state of existing with positive beliefs, the sure anticipation of favorable results. Optimistic thinking is hopeful and encouraging. The mysteries of life and its incredible possibilities are what keep the flames of optimism burning. As Helen Keller put it, "Optimism is the faith that leads to achievement." It is faith in things yet to be seen, the goals not yet realized. Everyday your round is full of opportunity for optimism.

How can you achieve an optimistic perspective? Just like in golf, success is achieved one swing at a time. Every swing has its challenges, but it also has its possibilities. It's hard to play a bad game when you have a great attitude. You are going to make mistakes, sure, but never lose sight of the possibilities. Focus on the change you desire and then head that direction. Begin taking small steps toward cultivating habits of optimism.

Here is a good starting point. Make it a habit to look for the good in each moment of your day. There is no surer way to a life of optimism than keeping your eyes and ears ready to see goodness.

As Oscar Wilde so perfectly put it, "We may all be in the gutter, but some of us are looking at the stars."

Another simple way to keep your silver lining shiny is to practice gratitude. If you find yourself in a situation where it would be oh-so-easy to find the bad, force yourself to find things to be thankful for in that situation. There is always, always something to be thankful for. And just to throw in one more cheesy cliché, "Choose an attitude of gratitude!" Before your feet hit the floor in the morning, think of two or three things you a grateful for. And as you are falling asleep at night, begin listing in your head all the things during the day that you were thankful for. They can be basic: gas in your car, a warm coat, etc. Falling asleep with a thankful heart is an easy way to cultivate optimism.

Culture offers us little chance of an optimistic worldview; the realities of this world are challenging. You'd be at best blind or at worst disingenuous to make any other claim. A casual understanding of the global challenges we face as a modern culture may leave us feeling less than optimistic. Don't lose heart. Can you imagine the changes it would bring not only to our own lives but to the lives of our children and children's children if we started a new legacy of optimism?

And as if family legacy wasn't reason enough to quit your whining, the health benefits are pretty impressive. According to the Mayo clinic, some studies show that traits such as optimism and pessimism can affect many areas of your health and well-being. The positive thinking that usually comes with optimism is a key part of effective stress management.

And effective stress management is associated with many health benefits including:

- Increased life span
- Lower rates of depression
- Lower levels of distress
- Greater resistance to the common cold
- Better psychological and physical well-being
- Better cardiovascular health and reduced risk of death from cardiovascular disease
- Better coping skills during hardships and times of stress[1]

Better health means less doctor visits, which means less bills, which means more money in your pocket. So essentially, looking on the bright side of things actually saves you money. There are really no negatives to being positive. Having an optimistic outlook will improve your life and the lives of others.

Let me tell you a quick parable *adapted from* <u>The Star Thrower</u>, by Loren Eiseley.[2] There was an old man walking down the beach after the tide brought in literally thousands of starfish. The elderly gentleman knew the heat of the day would kill the amazing creatures, so he started picking up as many starfish as he could, carefully throwing them back to the safety of the seas. A young boy approached the man after observing his laborious actions and asked, "Sir, why are you throwing the fish back in the water? There are thousands of them. There are too many, you can't possibly make a difference." The wise gentleman reached down and picked up a single starfish and tossed it back in the water and said, "It made a difference to that one."

Pursuing a spirit of optimism not only improves your life, but the lives of everyone you come in contact with.

TAKEAWAY PRINCIPLES ON OPTIMISM:

1.   Focus on the change you desire and then head that direction. Begin taking small steps toward cultivating habits of optimism.

2.   Make it a habit to look for the good in each moment of your day. There is no surer way to a life of optimism than keeping your eyes and ears ready to see goodness.

3.   The positive thinking that usually comes with optimism is a key part of effective stress management. And effective stress management is associated with many health benefits.

SIMPLE STEPS:

1.   Choose to find one good thing in every situation.

2.   Make a list of things you are grateful for. Keep one copy in your car and one by your bed. Add to it regularly.

3.   Surround yourself with happy people.

RECOMMENDED READING:

- *The Power of Positive Thinking by <u>Dr. Norman Vincent Peale</u>*
- *The Art of Optimism: Your Competitive Edge by Jim Stovall*
- *Relentless Optimism: How a Commitment to Positive Thinking Changes Everything by Darrin Donnelly*

WELL THAT'S INTERESTING . . .

In Japan, there is a tradition for golfers who get a hole-in-one to throw a party and give gifts to their friends and family as a way of sharing their good luck. This has led to a boom in sales of 'hole-in-one insurance,' whereby golfers pay a premium so that if they do score this wonder shot, a company will cover the cost of their celebrations![3]

NOTES

HOLE #8: COACHABILITY

NEVER STOP LEARNING

I never played a round when I didn't learn something new about the game.
—Ben Hogan

Golf teaches us life-giving principles for course management. You must be willing to live in a state of learning, because every opportunity is an opportunity for growth. Here's where I'd like to introduce the simple concept of coachability. Being coachable means you're open to listening to feedback, able to receive constructive criticism without taking it personally, and willing to take a look at your own performance in order to improve it.

This obviously not only applies on the golf course, but in every walk of life. Those who choose instruction and are receptive will position themselves for success. Being coachable isn't reserved for the formative years only, great golfers are always learning. Greatness has an innate hunger for information, technique, and application.

For the sake of comparison let's look at what being coachable is not:

- Thinking you are right
- Being unwilling to learn different ways of doing things
- Being negative or pessimistic

- Putting others down
- Being disrespectful to others' opinions
- Being unable to self-reflect

A winning pursuit has less to do with talent or gifting and more to do with a willingness to learn. Without it, players never reach anywhere near their potential. There is no sadder commentary on a life than that of squandered potential. This waste is primarily due to an unwillingness to entertain sound teaching due to pride, fear, laziness, or stubbornness. Those who gain notoriety and make it to the top will only stay at the top if they are teachable. This applies to every age. If you don't stay the course of learning, you will quickly add strokes to your game.

Here are some guidelines for making sure you are a teachable individual:

1. **Battle that nasty spirit that demands to always be right.**

If you desire to create an attitude that automatically defaults to learning, you must battle selfishness and ultra-sensitivity. It's difficult to find "right" if you insist that you are never wrong. Too much ego will kill your talent. It is also a little dangerous to insist on always being right; arrogance always precedes humiliation. Remember that it's better to choose humility over humiliation. Don't stunt your growth by thinking you know everything. Be willing to listen to others.

2. **Recognize the need to give up control.**

To enjoy the best of the game of golf you must be willing to submit and surrender control. Submission isn't a weakness; it is a willingness to yield to truth. A submissive individual will gladly accept truth whether it feels good or not. In an article for Forbes magazine on being coachable, August Turak shared this concept, "We implicitly insist that we will only give up control once we have seen results. In fact, we only get results if we are willing to give up control. Unwillingness to surrender control is the single biggest reason for the lamentable fact that most authentic change is precipitated by a crisis. Ironically, the reason why most of us need a coach in the first place is to learn how to give up control."[1]

3.   Be willing to learn at all times and from everyone!

Greatness resides next door. Every person you will bump into today can teach you something. Age is irrelevant, education is immaterial, and socio-economic status plays no role. Your new and acquired valuable insight can come from the man who lockers next to you at the club, it might be the girl in front of you at Starbucks, it could even come from the kid who is drying your car at the car wash. Just humbly open your eyes to learning. We all have amazing knowledge and unique perspectives, so learn from those around you.

4.   Take some time for some self-examination.

Be brutally honest with yourself about your failings. Then ask those who love you to be honest about where you are failing also. Honesty is the only way that you can work to improve your weaknesses with a teachable spirit. It certainly takes courage to consider your failings. Push yourself in areas that need improvement. Remember the Chinese Proverb, "He who asks a question remains a fool for five minutes. He who does not ask remains a fool forever." One final warning: Do not surround yourself with people who are not teachable. You become who you run with!

5.   Think outside the box.

Be willing to seek out unconventional avenues to travel in your pursuit of knowledge. Think of areas where you would like to improve. Whether it's your golf game, your parenting skills, your French—whatever it may be, seek out ways to improve those areas. It could be a class or a YouTube video. We have an endless world of information at our fingertips on any subject you can think of. Use it. I have tried to include at least one recommended book at the end of each chapter in case there is a specific area you need some concentrated growth in. It is astounding how much you can grow by simply reading a book. The ideas will be planted there regardless of how slow you read or how long it takes you to finish. Not a reader or think you have no time? Try listening to audiobooks. You can find just about any book in an audio version these days to download on your phone. Listen in your car, at the gym, or while you are working in the yard. Podcasts are also a great way of being entertained and getting information all at the same time. You could use a travel opportunity as a way to grow and learn. Sometimes simply the act of doing something new is the education itself.

Having a teachable spirit can create unexpected opportunities and also allow you to learn from others' mistakes. It doesn't always feel good to be instructed. While it may be humbling at times, mastering the art of coachability will put you in a class above the rest and will enrich your life and relationships. This learning journey creates significant rewards. The value of knowledge, truth, humility, and wisdom are immeasurable. So, take some time to invest in yourself.

TAKEAWAY PRINCIPLES ON COACHABILITY:

1. Being coachable means you're open to listening to feedback, able to receive constructive criticism without taking it personally, and willing to take a look at your own performance in order to improve it.

2. A winning pursuit has less to do with talent or gifting and more to do with a willingness to learn. Without it, you can never reach anywhere near their potential.

3. Having a teachable spirit can create unexpected opportunities and also allow you to learn from others' mistakes.

SIMPLE STEPS:

1. The next time someone suggests to you a new way to do something, even if you think its wrong, try it. It will create a shift in your way of interacting with people.

2. Try only saying "thank you" when people offer criticisms.

3. Learn something new that makes you a bit uncomfortable. Painting, tennis, woodworking, whatever you are not already good at. Sign up for a class and go in with a humble attitude ready to learn as much as you can.

RECOMMENDED READING:

- *Be Coachable: Tools and Tips from a Top Executive Coach* by Jill Chiappe

WELL THAT'S INTERESTING . . .

While we are on the subject of coaching and learning new things, let's take a lesson from Ben Hogan, and see if there is "something new" you may have not known about the game . . . [2]

- The word "caddy" comes from the French word for student, *cadet*, which is pronounced cad-DAY.
- There are 336 dimples on a regulation golf ball.
- The term "birdie" comes from an American named Ab Smith. While playing a round in 1899, he played what he described as a "bird of a shot," which became "birdie" over time.
- St. Andrews Golf Course was established in 1552.
- Three shots under par on a hole is called an "Albatross" or "Double Eagle."
- The largest bunker in the world is Hell's Half Acre on the 585-yard 7th hole of the Pine Valley Course in New Jersey.
- Balls travel significantly further on hot days.

NOTES

NOTES

HOLE #9: PRIORITIES

THE NON-NEGOTIABLES

Keep close count of your nickels and dimes, stay away from whiskey, and never concede a putt.
—Sam Snead

Every player's got to find his balance between ambition and sanity. Now, were major championships my focus? Yes. Where they my sole focus in life? No—my family was always before that. Could I have worked harder and won more majors? Probably. Could I have driven myself crazy doing it? Absolutely.
—Jack Nicklaus

In golf, the honor of hitting first is awarded to the player that set the standard on the previous hole. He gets priority. This participant has earned the right to lead his pairings. Rarely is this rule discounted. As you know, it really doesn't matter if you are in the midst of a PGA event or if you are a weekend player, this edict is of greatest importance.

A priority is something that is given special attention. It is something that is important to you that is a non-negotiable. If it is optional, it is not a priority; if it is up for discussion, it is not a priority. Priorities are not preferences. Priorities have conviction, preferences leave wiggle room. Priorities are simply rules we put into play as we manage our life's course.

They determine the standard you live by. The great part is *you* define them, you determine their order.

A priority in life is like clubbing first on any tee box. Any individual with their priorities in order will always hit first. Those who prioritize their life outhit other competitors consistently. Why? They are ready, they have prepared themselves, they have something they believe in and are disciplined enough to do whatever it takes to act in accordance to their belief system.

There is no other game where priority is greater than on the green. Listen to what Jordan Spieth said, "Look at the putt from behind the hole. Everyday players almost never do this. They should! Your eyes will take in information about the slope. Sometimes you'll find that your initial read was incorrect." Spieth said study your shot from every angle. Don't just look at life from the easiest vantage point. Climb the hill. Take your time. Examine the situation, read the green. Everyone starts with great intention and energy. Winners stay focused on their goals and the priorities needed to finish strong. Spend some time thinking about what you consider your life's priorities. Make a list. For example, spending time with your family, being excellent at your job, staying healthy, etc. It's hard to invest in your priorities if you don't know what they are.

Circumstances help shape your priorities. Nothing stretches an individual's commitment to their priorities like dealing with life. Circumstances are like hazards on the golf course. They take you places that can be dangerous to your score. Some circumstances can be thrown in your path you would have never dreamt of. They stretch you and cause you to reevaluate your agenda and adjust your shot. Many circumstances, however, are simply a result of our actions and behaviors. We often blame our circumstances on factors that, in reality, are avoidable. For the most part, your way of living is your choice. If it is unhealthy, change it. When you face trying circumstances, you may be *forced* to renegotiate some things to survive. Don't be so rigid or legalistic in your priorities that you damage your future or the future of those you love. You have to find balance. Too many people just hack their way through the hindrances. But when your priorities are set in place by your convictions and beliefs, then you can work through life's trying circumstances in a way that produces growth and healing. Evaluate your circumstances, follow your convictions, and then establish your priorities.

As a person of faith, I believe that our Creator has wonderful plans for each of us. His ways are never to harm us. Only plans for hope for your future (Jeremiah 29:11). When you are disappointed by an occasion that doesn't go the way you hoped, remember this: if that great plan is not God's best for your life, just imagine how good His plan will be. With this perspective, you learn patience and endurance. There are huge things happening all working in your best interest. Make big plans and establish the rules for reaching your goals. Then be flexible. Many things will affect your priorities; your spouse will shape or sharpen your priorities, your children, your job. Consider how the people you lead will help shape you and consider how you are shaping them. Trust God's plan and God's timing.

Continually invest your time and energy into your priorities. To "shore up" means to prop or provide support. This expression was first used to define a beam or timber used to strengthen or reinforce. Every day, pressure mounts against your priorities, so support your beliefs, goals, and objectives with focused attention. Take inventory of your priorities often. Ask yourself if are you investing time in what is non-negotiable. Keep in mind that your priorities will shift just as the seasons in your life do. That is natural. But continue to take stock.

Everyone's priorities are personal. However, can I make one suggestion. I would ask you to consider making radical changes in daily routines in order to attain a healthy lifestyle. Create margin in your schedule so that there is space to take care of you. Shape new priorities that strengthen your health. This is so essential. The body you reside in is miraculous. Value your health so much that it becomes a main priority. If you are unhealthy it is impossible to give proper attention to anything else. Begin today to pave a better existence not only for you but for those you influence and those you take care of.

TAKEAWAY PRINCIPLES ON PRIORITIES:

1.   Priorities are not preferences. A priority is something that is given special attention. It is something that is important to you that is a non-negotiable.

2.   Realize circumstances help shape your priorities. And your priorities will change in different seasons of life.

3.   Make your health a priority.

SIMPLE STEPS:

1.   Prioritize your life. Make a list of the things that are most valuable to you. Order them by number as to their importance. Be very honest with your list. Intentionally invest your best energy in the most important ones.

2.   Start to organize your life. Disorganization will cause you to invest energy needed to keep your priorities. If health is a priority, and you have chosen to go to the gym in the morning, organize your evening so you can get to the gym easily.

3.   Make your priorities public. Share them with a trusted friend or family member. Accountability is a powerful tool.

RECOMMENDED READING:

- *Younger Next Year: A Guide to Living Like 50 Until You're 80 and Beyond by Chris Crowley and Henry S. Lodge MD*
- *The Seven Pillars of Health: The Natural Way to Better Health for Life by Don and Mary Colbert*

WELL THAT'S INTERESTING . . .

Phil Mickelson, a champion since childhood and the winner of forty-two PGA Tour events, including five major championships, shocked the world when he announced that he would not be competing in the 2017 US Open in Wisconsin. Instead, he attended his daughter's high school graduation in California, where she gave the valedictorian speech. It marked the first time since 1993 that he missed this tournament. He had played in twenty-three consecutive US Opens.

Rickie Fowler said of Mickelson, "I think the decision shows what kind of person Phil is, that he understands that there are more bigger things in life than golf. Yeah, it's a major, and yeah, he wants a US Open. But he's obviously making family his priority."[1]

NOTES

THE TURN: REST

I don't know about you but I am always ready for the turn. The turn in golf represents the break between the front nine holes and the final nine yet to be played. Several things take place during the brief reprieve. You get out of the elements. Depending on the season you cool down or warm up physically. You restock for the journey yet ahead. Physical needs are met, phone calls returned, and nutritional needs to sustain you are acquired. A seasoned golfer will make equipment changes if necessary. Some golfers will take a moment and seek counsel, reflecting back on previous holes played, looking forward to what is yet to come. Others take pleasure in recalling the enjoyable or humorous times shared with fellow competitors. Whatever the case may be, intentionally spending a few minutes to recuperate is helpful.

The turn is important and at every level necessary. Why? A moment of retreat is healthy to our journey. You have to find rest, both physical and emotional. If you are a go-getter intent on significant living, you are most likely a busy person. Which makes "the turn" even more significant. Successful people desire to live, breathe, and appreciate every waking moment. Life starts early and goes late. That being the case somewhere in the midst of life's round a break is necessary. You have to find rest. Too many of us suffer from burn out from not taking care of ourselves. This does no good for us or the people we love. Remember, "You can't draw water from an empty well."

Some of you may be laughing at my suggestion of taking a break. "My life never slows down!" Your time is consumed at a frenzied pace. I understand that what you need to accomplish in a very brief amount of time may be considerable. This break is just time spent differently, its time spent taking care of yourself and refueling.

So, I would like to challenge readers to schedule a daily turn. At some point in the midst of your day, just rest for a moment. The benefits are enormous. A turn will assist you as you reload, rededicate, and reinvigorate. This intentional time allows you to reflect and evaluate. A quick recharge can persuade you to persevere for the remainder of the journey at hand. I am convinced a daily turn will keep you in the game physically, emotionally and spiritually. It's healthy and can certainly be enjoyable. Think of simple ways to allow yourself to recharge: a walk at lunch, ten minutes of afternoon meditation, a quick power nap, a simple activity that recharges you, or reading something of interest. You can accomplish a lot in a little time if you are willing and creative.

Also consider adding a break for yourself each year. I know some of you are thinking to yourselves that you haven't had a vacation in ten years. Well then take one. Heck, take two. I'm not saying you have to spend a month in Bora Bora. I'm just saying you will function so much better if you take a break every now and then,

You'll be surprised by how productive you can be after spending some time taking care of yourself. There are a million opportunities to create a dedicated turn. Whatever the case, make it happen. Well, are you ready for the back nine? Your "turn" is over.

HOLE #10: DISCIPLINE

THE ART OF SELF-CONTROL

Golf has always been a game where you have to control both ends of the club.
—Matt Kuchar

The great golfers all seem to possess a sense of fearlessness, living confidently in the present. But how can you be confident in a game where the smallest deviations can wreak havoc? Confidence is born of discipline. When you've done something a million times or have spent endless hours perfecting a shot . . . that's discipline. I've studied the approach thoroughly. Good golfers rely on their disciplined preparation; execution becomes second nature.

The tenth hole is often pivotal to the match. The front nine are behind you, and the back nine offer a fresh start. New goals will be set. At this point, you either evaluate exactly what you need to do to remain in the lead or consider what you need to do to get back on track. Discipline begins in the mind, but is lived out in action. To right the course takes a cognitive decision to discipline yourself.

Discipline may be the toughest principle we have covered. The Merriam-Webster dictionary first defines it as punishment—ouch. And facets of this concept may seem like punishment. But once you settle in, a disciplined life can become habitual and feel natural. And when you acclimate yourself to the rigors of discipline, these habits create momentum. It requires large amounts of self-control. But the greater the resolve, the less discipline feels like punishment. Every day you swing—mentally, emotionally, and physically. That's discipline. You make it a priority. A good golfer has accepted this routine and relishes the rigors. He knows that excellence achieved isn't a matter of chance, it is a matter of choice. The winning choice requires long-term discipline without exception. If you would add a measure of discipline to your routine in critical areas you would witness improvement in your score, in your health, in your relationships, and on and on. Discipline leads to incredible accomplishment and satisfaction. And nothing quite compares to the delight you feel when you accomplish something of value.

One of life's greatest challenges is overcoming "fast and easy." Too many people have fallen prey to a life of ease. Society is partially the culprit. Easy work, fast food, easy relationships, fast entertainment, the list could go on and on. We want things now and we want them to be easy to attain. This is when we truly have to practice self-control. Self-control and discipline go hand in hand. You cannot have one without the other. You will have to learn to say no to yourself sometimes. Don't get me wrong, I am grateful for all of life's comforts. I just wonder if the opulence of our time has made us into undisciplined, unintentional people. Intent is a measurable, fundamental desire to get things done! Intent is the foremost ingredient in disciplined living. Living intentionally requires introspecting to figure out what needs to change in your life and the discipline and self-control to accomplish it. If you know what you need to do you should do it! Find a way to see discipline with the value it deserves. Discipline generates opportunity. Sure, it is a more difficult lifestyle to that of ease, but it creates opportunity for victory.

I have this crazy thing I have done for many years that helps me in the area of self-discipline. I call it the "Earn the Right To" principle. Here's how it works: I must invest before I indulge. If I have some tasks that I need to perform around the house (like doing the dishes), I attempt to do them before I indulge in another more enjoyable activity (like working in my woodshop). Or I earn the right to watch a movie on the couch by cutting our back forty. I earn the right to my wife's amazing desserts by getting my workouts in. Basically, I practice discipline before I reward myself. I do the hard tasks so that I can more fully enjoy the activities I love. Discipline simply earns you the right to enjoy.

Success in life depends on the investment of your best energy. In other words, do the hard stuff first! If at all possible, attempt to accomplish the tough tasks when you are at your finest. Do you recall this advice, "Do it, do it right, do it right now"? It may be dated but it remains a powerful truth. I know if I wait or put things off I probably will at best be mediocre or at worst ineffective. Don't procrastinate on the hard stuff. Get it out of the way. Your daily agenda should include time to accomplish life's challenging tasks using your best energies. When is your best energy? It is different for everyone. For me it's early in the morning. That may not work for you. You may have children that require attention at that time. For some, your schedule is truly maxed out. Every moment is taken. Listen, I get it. Every season of life is different, so it is up to you to figure out what works best. And the busier you are the greater discipline is required. But work to find discipline that aligns with your priorities.

We have talked about having the discipline to accomplish things, so now let's spend a just a bit on having the self-control *not* to do things. Such as eating that second helping, getting mad at another driver and giving them a number one hand gesture, storming away from the monopoly board because you are losing (oh, just me?), having just one more drink, and on and on. I am not a psychologist, so I will not speak on addiction, but there are areas of our lives where we are prone to slip. And usually we have a pretty good idea of what those areas are. You may need to spend a few days self-evaluating if you are unsure. Once you have decided which areas those are, come up with a game plan to help encourage discipline and maintain self-control. If you struggle with road rage, practice mindfulness and play relaxing music. If you are prone to over indulge during meals, try being ahead of the game and drink a full glass of water prior to eating or use a smaller plate for portions. Figure out what you struggle with and come up with a plan. Disciplined people don't necessarily have stronger wills, they have stronger plans.

Wherever you find yourself in life, discipline and self-control are necessary. The more goals you have, the greater the discipline required. I believe you should be devoted to discipline at every stage of life. It will land you in the winner's circle every time!

Takeaway Principles on Discipline:

1. Confidence is born of discipline. When you've done something a million times or have spent endless hours perfecting your craft, you gain confidence.

2.   Discipline leads to incredible accomplishment and satisfaction. And nothing quite compares to the delight you feel when you accomplish something of value.

3.   Success in life depends on the investment of your best energy. In other words, do the hard stuff first! If at all possible, attempt to accomplish the tough tasks when you are at your finest.

4.   Disciplined people don't necessarily have stronger wills, they have stronger plans.

SIMPLE STEPS:

1.   Are you presently engaged in health-oriented disciplines? If so, list them out. If not, what is a small form of exercise you can begin with.

2.   Try incorporating the "Earn the Right To" principle in one area of your life. Watch for personal growth and improvement.

3.   Make a list of two tasks you do not like to do. Paying bills, laundry, etc. Pick a time when you think you have your most energy and try accomplishing those tasks then. Does it make it easier?

RECOMMENDED READING:

- *Make Your Bed: Little Things That Can Change Your Life...And Maybe the World by Admiral William H. McRaven*
- *Tools of Titans: The Tactics, Routines, and Habits of Billionaires, Icons, and World-Class Performers by Tim Ferriss*

WELL THAT'S INTERESTING . . .

I am not sure we can discuss discipline or self-control without mentioning the fine art of club killing. How easy is it to conjure up an image of a golfer losing control and chucking his golf club. Let's spend just a moment paying homage to a few of the greatest club abusers of all time.

- Tommy Bolt, AKA Terrible Tommy, was so known for filling the air with flying shafts that in 1957 the PGA of America instituted the so-called "Tommy Bolt Rule," which established fines for thrown implements. The day after the rule became official, Bolt launched a putter heavenward. Supposedly, he wanted to be the first man fined under "his" rule.

- Ben Curtis believed, "Destroying a club is almost healthy sometimes . . . You have to have a release. You play with fire out there, and a little bit of a release keeps the fire under control."

- Bobby Jones was a serial club abuser especially in his younger years. In a famous display at Brae Burn Country Club in 1917, after shanking a shot, Jones began throwing clubs and balls in all directions as the stunned crown looked on gasping.

- Paul Goydos said, "If you don't feel like taking out your anger on a club from time to time, you're probably not doing it right."

- Gene Sarazen once admitted "a bad shot was something to drive me into a tantrum, with the result that my reputation for club-throwing somewhat exceeded my prestige as a golfer." Sarazen had imagination as well. Reportedly, after one particularly perplexing round of wayward short putts, he placed the defective putter into a vise and sawed it into three sections.

- David Feherty admits to running over his clubs with his car after triple-bogeying the final hole to lose the 1981 Irish National PGA Championship. "I drove over them lengthwise so that I got all of them from grip to clubhead," he says. "Unfortunately, I left my watch in there."[1]

NOTES

HOLE #11: PERSEVERANCE

THE GRIT AND THE GRIND

I've won as many golf tournaments hitting the ball badly as I have hitting the ball well.
—Jack Nicklaus

Grind is a word often used in golf circles. It represents the tedious stretch of the round that requires incredible energy and perseverance. These holes sometimes seem more like a chore you must endure. Many a player resigns due to the rigors of the grind. One thing is certain, successful golfers understand the battle and have the grit it takes to continue on.

On and off the course we will struggle. Would you be described as having grit? Are you intimidated by difficulty? By nature, humanity desires the path of least resistance but little is learned on that broad path. Amazing experience and maturity can be acquired on the difficult roads. Resolve and perseverance will be essential. Just consider all the lessons learned on the golf course as it relates to the tough stretch of the journey. You can take a month of lessons and never learn what you learn as you grind your way down the stretch. The value of that grind is immeasurable. Who you are during those times is usually a good indicator of your character.

Opportunities can often be found in the drudgery. And these opportunities aren't realized at times when we are complaining. Too often we agonize over the burdens of life, when there are rewards found in the effort. This is when focused, goal-oriented people shine. The real you is on stage for everyone to see. Inspire those who travel alongside of you by your perseverance. Now is the time to confidently serve others and to exemplify leadership qualities. The grind can't be about you and your challenges exclusively. It's a powerful time to invest in others.

Too many people quit on their dreams during seasons of difficulty. Just for a moment look at your potential. The potential for success is ever-present. We often give in too soon. You have to have grit to keep moving on. William James, America's first professor of psychology, said, "Most people never run far enough in their first wind to find they have a second. Give your dreams all you have and you will be amazed at the energy that comes out of you." Your potential will be challenged, but if you persevere, you will be amazed at what you can do.

Don't be discouraged if you don't think of yourself as someone having grit. Grit is something that can be learned. If it is not strength of yours, fear not, it can be. It is like anything else, it takes practice. There are many simple ways to start cultivating grit and the first is belief in your ability to accomplish whatever it is you are doing. The brain is moldable. Research has shown time and time again that the brain can be changed (research neuroplasticity to learn more). So, choose to believe. Also, the more you accomplish, the more grit you have. So, set some small goals and start knocking them out. In time, the goals will grow and so will your grit. There are many great articles, podcasts, and books on grit. Take some time to further your research.

People were designed to find their worth and value in their hard work. So, don't resent the grind. Even in the most rigorous of occasions, you must persevere. L. Thomas Holdcroft, English dramatist and author, said, "Life is a grindstone. Whether it grinds you down or polishes you up depends on you." If you quit in the jaws of the journey, you will regret it. The holes yet to be played need your complete attention and resolve. When you persevere people will see more than a polished game, they will see a polished you.

TAKEAWAY PRINCIPLES ON PERSEVERANCE:

1.   The potential for success is ever present in the grind. But we often give up just before we reach it.

2.   Perseverance/grit is something that can learned.

SIMPLE STEPS:

1.   Think about seasons of difficulty in your life. How did you respond? Did you persevere through them? Is there anything you would do different?

2.   Go to Angela Duckworth's website and take the "Grit Test."

3.   If you are building up your grit, make a list of small goals you would like to accomplish. If you feel perseverance is a strength, then right down a big crazy goal that no one would ever believe you could do and go prove them wrong.

RECOMMENDED READING:

- *Grit: The Power of Passion and Perseverance by Angela Duckworth*
- *Grit to Great: How Perseverance, Passion, and Pluck Take You from Ordinary to Extraordinary by <u>Linda Kaplan Thaler</u>*

WELL THAT'S INTERESTING . . .

At the age of two, D.J. Gregory's parents were told that their youngest of three children would never walk. Because of cerebral palsy, he would be in a wheelchair for the rest of his life. After learning to be mobile by sliding around with his arms, D.J. grew to walk with the aid of a walker with wheels, and then with two canes, and then eventually one.

At the age of nine, D.J. started playing golf. "My swing is a self taught swing. I swing one handed." When asked how his golf game was, he replied with a smile, "It sucks." But for D.J., golf is more than numbers. It's a love and a passion. It has taught him perseverance and to chase after what you want. Including earning a master's in sports management.

In 2008, D.J. set a personal goal to walk every hole of every tournament in the PGA tour that year. Something the pros do not even do. He walked 3,256 holes. More than 900 miles. He fell more than two dozen times, but kept on walking. He said, "You know if I fall, I fall. It's just another challenge. I'm gonna fall, it's just the way it is. But you get back up. And you learn from your mistakes . . . I will never give up on anything. Or let anyone tell me no."

Now visiting forty-five to fifty PGA Tour events annually, Gregory covers more than 1,000 miles while walking nearly 3,500 holes, including playoffs. "It's what I do," Gregory said, "and I love what I do."

In late 2009, D.J. Gregory formed the Walking For Kids Foundation, which allows PGA Tour professionals and sports fans the opportunity to support several children's charities. Throughout the PGA Tour season, players pick a tournament they are participating in and pledge money for each eagle and birdie they make that week. D.J. also holds a golf tournament each year where golf enthusiasts have the opportunity to play with PGA Tour players, celebrities, and with D.J. himself. The WFKF also receives numerous donations from people through the country who are inspired by D.J. and want to participate in his mission to help children.

When asked about the starting the foundation, D.J. Gregory commented, "After some thought and discussions, I have decided to start my own foundation and raise money for children's charities from coast to coast. The goal of my foundation will be to raise money and help children of all ages realize and live out their dreams and goals, as I did in 2008."[1]

NOTES

Hole #12: Humility

Leading from Behind

The only time my prayers aren't answered is on the golf course.
–Dr. Billy Graham

The ebb and flow in golf is one of the many alluring attributes of the game. You can be flying high one moment with the confidence of a champion and in the next moment be ready to hang up the clubs in total humiliation following a complete implosion. When describing the emotions involved in golf, Mac O'Grady expressed it this way, "One minute you are bleeding. The next minute you are hemorrhaging. The next minute you are painting the Mona Lisa." One thing is certain, if you plan to excel in the greatest game ever invented, you must deal with the emotional lows, and so it goes with life. There will be humiliating experiences at some point; therefore, humility is required.

During my son's senior year in high school, his golf team was vying for a state championship. It was the final day of the tournament. Needless to say, the teams were close and every swing was both calculated and critical. My boy had performed well on the front nine and took an under-par score into the turn. The tenth hole was a short par three with an elevated, sloped green. His first shot drifted slightly left, bounced on the green then rolled ever so slowly until it fell into the deep trap on the left side of the green. The closer we got to the green, it became apparent that it would take a very good sand wedge shot to even get out of the predicament. After surveying his shot, he made his decision. With outward confidence, he approached the ball and gave it his best. The height of the trap was the problem, however, and his sand wedge shot failed. The ball fell even closer to the wall of the trap. Three shots later, he decided to punch out in the opposite direction of the green to be free of this dreadful trap. The par three became a nine for him that day and two under went to four over par.

As a father, I thought I would literally implode. I am his protector, yet I was rendered helpless. You could even see the agony on his coach's face. The golfing community is truly a family and those observing my son's painful situation, even his competitors on that day, took no pleasure in what he was feeling. It was truly a humbling experience. You say, "that's golf." Yes, it is, and humbling experiences happen at some point to all who will participate. So, what will you do when trouble happens? My son fought back from the difficulty on number ten to shoot an even par for the round. He found a way that day to use the experience for good and excelled. To this day, we talk of lessons learned on number ten. Your pain can grow your game when you handle adversity with a humble spirit and resolve.

What about being humble when you win? It's a must. There are two kinds of pride we must deal with in this life. One is good, and one is bad. It's that simple. How can you tell between the two? Here is a great formula: Good pride always benefits others, and the bad pride serves self. Good pride is praiseworthy and is an appealing part of this game. Golf is a noble game created with character and integrity at is core. One can and should take pride in our fascinating sport. On occasion, unfortunately, the self-absorbed "bad pride" rears its ugly face. There is nothing humble about that. Praising others before yourself is not only true pride it is true humility.

If humility were superman, then entitlement would be kryptonite. Sadly, I think Tiger figured this out too late. Tiger Woods has experienced incredible highs and desperate lows. To claim Mr. Woods is in the top five players in history is not an understatement. He held the number one ranking in professional golf for a total of 545 weeks during his professional career. Only two golfers in history have won more tournaments than Tiger. However, he fell due to entitlement. His words not mine. His highly publicized infidelity cost him dearly. Here's the point: no one is immune. Tiger warned of the danger of entitlement when he said, "Money and fame made me feel I was entitled." He went on to say, "I was wrong and foolish." Entitlement says I have a license to act any way I see fit because of my gifting. It is essentially a free pass to do as you please, based on circumstances. Tiger was painfully humbled at his error and all areas of his life suffered from it. But that's not the end of the story, Tiger Woods worked hard and worked humbly, and, ten years after his last major win, he won the 2019 Masters. There is a strong lesson here, our legacy isn't in the mistakes that we make, but how we respond to those mistakes. Will you respond in humility or pride? Will you work humbly to meet your potential or will you crumble in defeat? You have the choice.

Let's talk about another humility killer: arrogance. Confidence is essential to shooting a good score on the golf course. Overconfidence or arrogance is an abuse of that attribute. It typically draws attention to you, rather than adding value to others. Selfishness is evident in the life of an overconfident person. Consider this: it really doesn't matter how good you are, how much you have accumulated, or what you believe you have mastered: there is someone, somewhere that is better, or wealthier, or more accomplished. Arrogance is neither attractive nor smart. Arrogance requires of a person something they will never be able to deliver—perfection. You can't expect perfection, only excellence. Jordan Spieth talks often of the fallacy of perfection. He advises players to "manage their misses" well. Spieth went on to say that the goal is just about trying to limit the mistakes. Young Mr. Spieth, wise beyond his years, teaches players to not aim for perfection, but to minimize errors and to focus on strategies that overcome errant shots. So, get over yourself. Embrace humility before you are humbled.

Humility requires admitting your mistakes, learning from them, and using your experiences to serve others. Only humility can clean up a big mess. You will deal with inevitable scars, yes. But things can be straightened out. When you have a balanced emotional approach, it results in humility. So, use all your experiences for good: encourage others, tell your story, and help by becoming a leader from behind. It is so wasteful to lose the emotional lessons learned from mistakes, instead turn them into something great. Your victories are a good story to tell. And, in many cases, so are your defeats.

I am a firm believer that a humble stance is the position of greatest possible change and learning. Why not assume a different attitude and investigate the greatness that is all around you? This understanding is healthy humility.

Takeaway Principles on Humility:

1.   There will be humiliating experiences at some point in your life; therefore, humility is required. Your pain can help you grow in every area when you handle adversity with a humble spirit and resolve.

2.   There are two kinds of pride we must deal with in this life. One is good and one is bad. Good pride always benefits others, and the bad pride serves self.

3.   Arrogance is neither attractive nor smart. Arrogance requires of a person something they will never be able to deliver—perfection.

SIMPLE STEPS:

1.   Examine how you behave when you win and when you lose. Which areas need some tweaking? Make a commitment to win quietly and lose with a smile.

2.   Make it a habit to always turn the spotlight on others.

RECOMMENDED READING:

- *Humility: The Secret Ingredient of Success by* <u>*Pat Williams*</u>

WELL THAT'S INTERESTING . . .

I found this little limerick on the lesson of being humble:

When his short putt just slipped by the hole

In frustration he lost all control

And gouged out the green

On number fourteen,

Like something carved out by a mole.

Embarrassed, he wished to implore

His etiquette had been heretofore

Exemplary in kind.

So we're more inclined

To speak of this event . . . nevermore.[1]

NOTES

Notes

HOLE #13: FUN

TIME TO LIGHTEN UP

Golf isn't supposed to be work. It's to have fun.
—Moe Norman

"We don't stop playing because we grow old; we grow old because we stop
playing."
—George Bernard Shaw

Both golf and life should be fun. Fun doesn't end when you graduate sixth grade. I admit, we have discussed some very heavy topics to this point in the book. Life, just like golf, has some serious junctures that have to be met with serious preparation. If you are committed to significant living, then training, groundwork, and even homework are all a part of the journey—but we cannot leave out the fun.

Some see life as all business and no play. Some see golf through the same lens. Now I am not saying business can't be done on the golf course. On the contrary, I think it's a great idea as long as you remember that golf was created to bring joy, not stress. If you can take care of business while enjoying the game of golf, that is awesome. What a great way to have fun, build relationships, compete, and take care of business all in one. That's quality multitasking there.

Think about what you truly love about golf. What drew you to the sport? There are simple joys to be found that are a bonus to a great day of competition. I'll tell you what I love. For starters I love being outside. I really enjoy the outdoors, especially the warm days of summer. And you get that smoking hot golfer's tan. There is nothing like bronzed legs and pasty ankles to make a woman swoon. I also love walking so I get five miles worth of nature every time I play. On occasion, I need a good cigar when I play some golf. It's life at its best.

Now think about life. What do you love to do? If you are reading this book, most likely your first thought was golf. Do you have fun playing? What else do you consider fun? Whatever it is, get some more of it into your life. The benefits far outweigh your busy schedule.

Cortisol, known as the "stress hormone" or the "fight or flight hormone" spikes to unhealthy levels when we're stressed. It's intended to save our lives in do-or-die situations; however, at low levels of stress (when there's nothing to fight or flee) cortisol can cause weight gain and can even inhibit the body's ability to fight off infection and heal itself. Hello heart attack. Having fun and taking the time to play reduces cortisol levels. And then there is our friend serotonin. Having fun increases serotonin levels. Serotonin is a chemical that regulates many of our most basic processes, including sleep patterns, memory, body temperature, and mood. Doing activities, you enjoy that help you relax and connect with others naturally increases the body's serotonin levels. Reduced cortisol levels and increased serotonin levels that come with having fun mean you'll enjoy a clearer mind and better memory, you will sleep more soundly and have an increase in energy levels.[1]

Forming meaningful connections with others is one of the most significant health benefits of having fun. Don't overlook this. As a pastor for many years, I have seen people that have been so into the business of life that they have missed out on the joy of relationships. I have counseled many that have made it to relational milestones yet failed at the abundant life spoken of in the gospel of John. What good is it to make it fifty years in marriage only to sum up the "golden" journey as painful? You desperately need fun in your relationships. If your power and prestige afford you a castle, don't exist alone in one part of the house.

As we finish up let's talk about the power of laughter. Laughing lightens our load. It changes our mood and can take the edge off of a serious situation in seconds. I know life is challenging. So is golf. It can make you want to cuss (Raymond Floyd said, "They call it golf because all the other four-letter words were taken"). But it can also make you laugh. I mean belly laugh. So, go with it. You become more positive and optimistic, more hopeful and engaged. We are friendlier, more attractive, and simply more alive. Engage in activities you enjoy, laugh, spend time with people that make you happy, and go have some fun!

TAKEAWAY PRINCIPLES ON FUN:

1. Make time to have fun. The benefits far outweigh your busy schedule.

2. Doing activities you enjoy that help you relax and connect with others naturally increases the body's serotonin levels. The reduced cortisol levels and increased serotonin levels that come with having fun mean you'll enjoy a clearer mind and better memory, you will sleep more soundly and have an increase in energy levels.

3.   Laughter truly is the best medicine. You become more positive and optimistic, more hopeful and engaged. We are friendlier, more attractive, and simply more alive.

SIMPLE STEPS:

1.   Take a few minutes to think of things you have fun doing. Now schedule one of them into your week.

2.   Laugh at stupid jokes. It still counts.

3.   If you are prone to saying no to invitations, start saying yes. There is life in community with others.

RECOMMENDED READING:

- *God Loves Golfers Best: The Best Jokes, Quotes, and Cartoons for Golfers by Ray Foley*

WELL THAT'S INTERESTING . . .

Now, we can't have fun without a few cheesy over used golf jokes . . .

- A golfer has one advantage over a fisherman.

- He doesn't have to produce anything to prove his story.

- What should you do if your round of golf is interrupted by a lightning storm?

- Walk around holding your 1-iron above your head, because even God can't hit a 1-iron!

- A golfer sliced a ball into a field of chickens, striking one of the hens and killing it instantly. He was understandably upset, and sought out the farmer. "I'm sorry," he said, "my terrible tee-shot hit one of your hens and killed it. Can I replace the hen?"

- "I don't know about that," replied the farmer, mulling it over. "How many eggs a day do you lay?"

- Two men were leaving church on a bright Sunday morning. "You know," said the first friend, "I can always tell who the golfers are in church." "How's that?" said his friend. "It's easy," he said. "You just look at who is praying with an interlocking grip."

- Wife: "I'm sick and tired of your obsession with golf!"

- Husband: "Why, is it driving a wedge between us?"

- If you golf on Election Day, be sure to cast an absent-tee ballot.

- Have a good round—may the fours be with you. [2]

NOTES

Hole #14:
Introspection

The Voices in Your Head

Hit the shot you know you can hit, not the one you think you should.
—Bob Rotella

Introspection isn't a word we use very often and can sometimes be confused with "inspection." Inspection is an outward look, introspection is an inward look. Success on the golf course and in life is much more than just looking good on the outside. The problem is, you can easily fool others by just focusing on the outward. Introspection, however, goes deeper and is much more detailed than just an outward look. It's a characteristic that is essential for success. Introspection is self-examination and requires asking questions of yourself. Essentially, is everything in alignment?

I love to watch serious golfers go through their rituals before they swing. They will intentionally survey their position: beginning with their feet, working their way up to their grip, and then finishing with their head placement before they strike. Going through the list is essential. It capitalizes on the endless hours of practice and preparation already invested in the pursuit of greatness. One minor flaw can and generally will affect the flight of the ball; little things make a difference in the outcome of the swing, so they check to make sure everything is aligned.

Have you ever driven a car that has alignment issues? It's not fun. You struggle to keep the vehicle on the road. The steering pulls in directions dangerous to your journey. You even damage your tires. Just like a car that isn't in alignment, an unexamined life finds itself in the same dangerous and precarious position. Too often we are pulled to the left or pushed to the right by our habits and actions that are destructive to our course, all due to misalignment. To manage your life, you must seek alignment. The questions we inquire of ourselves are similar to the questions we ask when on the golf course. Am I on track? Have I set my standards high enough that I can reach my goals and am I living in obedience to my priorities?

Introspection is not something that can just be done every now and then. Your natural tendencies are in a constant battle with your spirit. That deeply rooted hope to be who you were called, gifted, and designed to be isn't something you naturally drift into. It requires regular check-ups of your intentions and actions. Throughout the day you must take inventory. I once had the opportunity to manage a company that required a monthly inventory of its multi-million-dollar parts and equipment. I quickly learned that inventory is tough. It doesn't just ask; it tells, it orders, it demands. One thing was very evident: my staff and I were better qualified for our jobs because of the disciplined effort. We were better employees because we took stock of what was happening. The results outweighed the effort.

You have to take a good look at your life and ask yourself the tough questions. Are you living a full existence rather than just getting by? Are you making a difference in the lives of others? Asking the tough questions of yourself may also save your life. Taking the time to look deep and make adjustments can keep you from addictive behaviors. If you take the easy route and never introspect, you may find yourself in a life of mediocrity. Who wants that? When you require of yourself this discipline, you put yourself in a position to succeed. Asking yourself the tough questions is an important first step, but then you must listen. You must listen to the honest truth of the answers to the questions you are asking yourself. Humanity has a way of turning the volume down when it does not like what it hears. And it's gotten all too easy to distract yourself from internal issues. The frustrating part is you can't lie to the voice of truth. You can fool the outward, but the inward isn't buying it. And that is a good thing.

Let me run you through four voices you need to listen and respond to as you begin to introspect:

The Voice of Truth: Some call it your conscience. Whatever you call it, this voice speaks truth. The inner voice is your moral compass. You are designed with infinite potential and the inner voice reminds you of your course. At times it whispers. There are times when it screams! It can be annoying, inspiring or even soft and quiet. But no matter what, it speaks the truth. You may respond back to the inner voice of truth with defensive thoughts, and on rare occasions you may talk yourself out of truth. This voice has your best interest in mind. It calls you to a greater commitment. The inner voice never tires in its pursuits. It's combative, and it doesn't mind a little confrontational dialogue. Listen to it. And whatever you do, don't turn down the volume.

The Discontent Voice: You are aware that there is a war going on internally, aren't you? We call it the battle between the flesh and the spirit, good versus evil, or disciplined versus undisciplined living. When you don't listen to the voice of truth, you are filled with remorse or unhappiness. It undeniably saddens us when we choose a path in life that is counterproductive to our well-being. This is the voice of discontent. A healthy unhappiness or displeasure with the decisions you're making can catapult you to expect more of yourself and to achieve an even greater reward. This is healthy. Unhealthy is when negative self-talk creeps in keeps you from learning and moving on. It wants to replay every negative aspect and remind you of why you won't succeed. Don't listen. (If you are someone that struggles with negative self-talk please take the time to check out the recommended reading. It's a game changer.) Your success in golf and life requires being in tune with the discontent voice. It will help drive you to preparation and practice, and it will push you to make the changes necessary to stay on track.

The Successful Voice: You know what works and what doesn't. The voice of truth and the discontent voice aren't shy in their jobs; their task is clear. The successful voice is the offspring of the two. When your decisions lead you to become more of the person that you want to be, the successful voice applauds your progress. When you do something well or accomplish a goal, the successful voice gives you a golf clap. You feel proud and you hunger for more. The successful voice can be more prominent for those of us who have been encouraged and lifted up in our lives. But sadly, there are many who actually have never heard the successful voice. Whether through upbringing, environment, or your own unattainable standards you just have not found it. Listen, you will eventually burn out if you never recognize your accomplishments. You can also learn to hear the successful voice as you delight in others' victories as well as your own. The successful voice is there to affirm the positive decisions that the voice of truth and the discontent voice lead you toward, and it helps you rejoice in your accomplishments and victories. Crank the volume on this one.

THE HIGHER VOICE:

DISCLAIMER It is never my heart to push my beliefs. However, I want to share a little of my own story. So, I will write this final point, and describe a bit of my journey and share my faith. If that is not something you believe in or desire to learn about, just head up to the clubhouse and relax for a few minutes, then enjoy the next chapter.

Very early in life I realized there was Someone bigger than me who cared about me. There had to be more to my story than just happenstance. I came to understand God's love for me and the sacrifice He made by allowing His son Jesus to suffer and die on a cross. I trusted in this higher message and accepted this gracious gift of faith and salvation. Nothing compares to the position I now hold in the family of God. The Higher Voice is consistent and caring and now leads me and guides me. I gladly pay attention to His magnificent voice and cannot imagine doing life on my own. So, I will happily submit to His plans because I am convinced His heart for me is joy. He has proven His love over and over again. I would ask that you think about His higher call on your life. He loves you and has a great plan for your life. He can transform any circumstance and bring beauty from any situation. Please contemplate a relationship with Jesus Christ. I believe there is nothing more course-changing than Him.

Takeaway Principles on Introspection:

1.   Inspection is an outward look, introspection is an inward look.

2.   You have to take a good look at your life and ask yourself the tough questions. But don't stop there. Listen and make adjustments.

Simple Steps:

1.   Do you hear voices? (Don't laugh, I am being serious here.) In this chapter, I have defined them using various terminology. What descriptive terminology best describes the voices you hear?

2.   Asking the tough questions requires courage. Here are some directives to consider:

a.   Am I doing my best to live a life of integrity?

b.   Have I identified my strengths and weaknesses?

c.   What activity do I need to add to my life that will enhance my existence and take me in the direction of my goals? What things should I remove?

3.   Positive self-talk can help rewire the way you think. Take the time to search out some inspiration quotes that can help encourage you and remind you of what direction you want to be going. Keep them on hand for times when you need to shut down negative thoughts. Here is a favorite of our family's: "Today I will do what others won't, so tomorrow I can accomplish what others can't."

RECOMMENDED READING:

- *What to Say When You Talk to Yourself by Shad Helmstetter*
- *Seven Days in Utopia: Golf's Sacred Journey by <u>David L. Cook</u>*

WELL THAT'S INTERESTING . . .

Sometimes the voices in our head don't stay quiet. In the case of many golfers, they come out directed at their golf balls. Some have nice things to say, and, well, some don't. Either way, the insanity of talking to an inanimate object is perfectly normal on the course. Here is a short compilation of some colorful talk from a few of golf's well known:

- Zach Johnson likes to soothe his golf balls all Barry White style "Come on baby. Come on Baby."
- Bubba Watson speaks incoherently and likes grunt noises, "Mud ball. Mud ball. Mud ball. Uh. Uh. Uh."
- Ian Poulter has a partial potty mouth, "Eh. Sit there you bleep."
- Tiger Woods still can't kiss his mama with that mouth, "Bleep you, you bleeping bleep. Bleep. You bleeping bleep of a bleeper."
- Jordan Spieth talks to his golf balls on just about every hole. Begging for mercy is his usual tactic, "Aw jeez get over the water. Get over the water. Get. What, Ahhh."[1]

NOTES

HOLE #15: CAUTION

THE EDUCATION OF FAILURE

A golf ball can stop in the fairway, rough, woods, bunker, or lake. With five equally likely options, very few balls choose the fairway.
—Jim Bishop

A primary reason we pay attention to the principles covered in this book thus far is to minimize the errors we make out on the course. You have to do your best to avoid mistakes down the stretch because there is not always enough time to recover from them. However, there is always time to learn from them. There are hazards in golf and hazards in life and sometimes they are unavoidable. You will fail. You will make mistakes. That is inevitable. But you cannot let those mistakes define your self-image. The key to success is how quickly we convert failure into education and, ultimately, into lasting changes in behavior evidenced through caution.

Consideration of the past has great value. Stay in your experiences for a brief moment. Contemplate the cost of the mistakes in your round, but don't mentally stay there too long. Command your mind to move on to the task at hand. The value of the past can only be realized when you forget the mistake and remember the lesson.

Learning the lessons is not always easy, however. Especially if we are still wallowing in frustration and disappointment or nursing a bruised ego. There is nothing quite like embarrassment to hinder the growth process. Add to that resentment and hopelessness and it's enough to make you want to hide. A good way to get back on track is to evaluate what you might do differently next time. If you encounter a hazard, if you make a mistake, if you fail, learn from it. What are areas you could add more planning and preparation. How could you execute differently? What are things that were simply out of your control? These guidelines are a simple way to discover invaluable lessons. Also, be keenly aware of what lessons you can take away from the mistakes of others. It is infinitely less painful.

To confidently exist in the present requires the greatest of discipline. Humanity, by nature, tends to wallow in the past or even selfishly envy the future. We don't love the roadwork necessary to reach the pinnacle of the present— it's steep and uphill. Mistake-ridden rounds can affect your confidence. The final holes of any golf match require the greatest confidence. If you don't believe in your potential then you will relent easily, which is a big mistake in and of itself. You have great potential. Remember that your greatest talent is so much more powerful than your greatest fear. Don't let mistakes of the past cloud your aspirations for the future.

Some hazards are unavoidable. But some come with their own blinking neon signs, so be on your guard always. In life, careless blunders can dictate outcomes. Mistakes can blemish your legacy. Granted, mistakes will happen. They are often proof that you are trying. But you have to make a daily effort to make decisions you won't wish to erase later. I have used the following illustration before at speaking engagements, and to this day it remains a favorite. A pencil is typically made up of 90 percent lead for writing and 10 percent eraser. It was created to write infinitely more than it erases. Same for you. Write more, erase less. And if you do have to erase, rewrite it better. There is always grace for our mistakes. And if you want to live a life of influence, learning from your mistakes is vital.

Applying the lessons you learned from your mistakes results in maturity and significant living.

Concentration, intentionality, and focus are now the highest priorities. You will rely on your preparation and your desire to win. Hold yourself up to a disciplined standard. The past is where you have committed and learned the lessons. The finish is where the lessons are confidently and knowingly applied.

TAKEAWAY PRINCIPLES ON CAUTION:

1. The key to success is how quickly we convert failure into education and, ultimately, into lasting changes in behavior.

2. Be keenly aware of what lessons you can take away from the mistakes of others. It is infinitely less painful.

SIMPLE STEPS:

1. Identify potential hazards in your life. Take steps to avoid them.

2. Forgive yourself for previous mistakes made. Decide what you can learn from them. And then move on.

RECOMMENDED READING:

- *In Praise of Failure: The Value of Overcoming Mistakes in Sports and in Life by Mark H. Anshel*

WELL THAT'S INTERESTING . . .

Here are a few unique rules pertaining to hazards that you may have never heard before:

- If a ball comes to rest in dangerous proximity to a crocodile, another ball may be dropped *(Local rule at Jinja Golf Club, Uganda.)*
- If your ball lands within a club length of a rattlesnake you are allowed to move the ball *(Local rule at Glen Canyon GC in Arizona).*
- If your ball lands near a cactus you can wrap a towel around your arm or leg to protect yourself. But you cannot cover the cactus.
- If your ball gets imbedded in a piece of fruit, you must play the ball/fruit as it lies or declare it unplayable. [1]

NOTES

NOTES

HOLE #16: PERSPECTIVE

BATTLING YOUR FEAR

The mind messes up more shots than the body.
—Tommy Bolt

Of all the hazards, fear is the worst.
—Sam Snead

Knowing what you believe and why you believe it is tantamount to what your perspective will be in life. The word perspective has a Latin root meaning "look through" or perceive." It quite frankly means "a point of view." Perspective is a mental outlook on any situation; it is the lens through which we view life. You must take any circumstance and formulate a proper point of view. Balance is essential as you develop this point of view. When the balance is off, we may believe things that are untrue simply because our perspective is skewed. Perspective or putting something into perspective requires judgment and organizing your life as it relates to what is most important. Perspective is an equally essential on the golf course. Even at the very beginning when you find yourself at the tee box, perspective helps you find the approach that gives you the best chance of landing the ball in the proper fairway location.

Having the proper perspective can be critical. And one area that I believe perspective has an immense impact is how we handle fear. First let's talk about the difference between fear and caution. Fear is defined as a distressing emotion aroused by impending danger, evil, pain, etc., whether the threat is real or imagined; the feeling or condition of being afraid. Caution is defined as alertness and prudence in a hazardous situation; care; wariness. Do you see one major difference between the two? You can have fear in a situation even if the threat is imagined, based on your perspective. Do you get how powerful that is? We fear things that are not even real. A poplar acronym for fear is False Evidence Appearing Real. It is up to you to decide if a perceived threat or danger is real and you need to exercise caution. Or if there are no visible facts and fear is just an emotion stopping you from achieving something based on the unknown or the difficult.

It has been said that fear is the most powerful emotion known to humankind. More powerful even than love. It is an ancient feeling triggered in the most primitive part of our brain. So, we must learn how to gain the correct perspective on what our perceived fears are if we plan to conquer them and figure out how to use fear in our favor. Imagine what you could accomplish if you learned to harness one of the most powerful human emotions for your own benefit.

First let's recognize that fear often indicates that something big is about to happen. Yes, that can be scary. But it can also be amazing. Choose to believe the latter. Make fear your friend. Allow it to energize you. When you decide to ignore the fears and move forward, you gain mental strength. Even if you fail. You become stronger and wiser when you push past fear and fail. You also become more adventurous and courageous after the battle. Really the benefits of embracing fear are endless and impact every area of your life.

Let me conclude with this. Learn the difference between caution in your gut and fear in your head. You should have caution in unfamiliar situations. And you should have caution if you sense danger (i.e. snakes, tigers, politicians). Listen to your gut. Caution is absolutely exercised in a fearless life. That is healthy. But do not allow fear to override caution and stop you from achieving your goals and enjoying the best life has to offer.

"Caution is what causes you to look both ways before crossing the street. Fear is what keeps you frozen on the curb forever. You know the difference. You can feel it. If you're 'stuck' right now, you're probably into fear. Get out of there. You've already looked both ways. Now cross the street for heaven's sake. The cars have long since gone. The coast is clear. Your only obstacle now is your own mind." –Neale Donald Walsch

Takeaway Principles on Perspective:

1.   Knowing what you believe and why you believe it is tantamount to what your perspective will be in life.

2.   Fear often indicates that something big is about to happen.

3.   Learn the difference between caution in your gut and fear in your head.

Simple Steps:

1.   List out things you fear. Then decide if they are actually things you need to be concerned with.

2.   Write down one goal you have been too afraid to go after. Now write what your fears are in regard to the goal. Then map out a strategy to overcome any of the potential hazards. This is an exercise in breaking down fear.

RECOMMENDED READING:

- See Tim Ferriss' "7 Steps to Overcoming Fear" as Published in Entrepreneur.com. The TED talk is also on YouTube.[1]

WELL THAT'S INTERESTING . . .

You may have never heard of Moe Norman but he was considered one of the best ball strikers of all time. He won over fifty tournaments, shot 59 three times in tournaments, had nineteen holes-in-one and the straightness of his shots apparently had to be seen to be believed. There are people that still obsess over his technique and work to emulate his swing. Tiger Woods is quoted as saying, "Only two players have ever truly owned their swings, Moe Norman and Ben Hogan."

Karl Morris is the lucky owner of a true piece of golf history. It's "a simple piece of A4 paper which has written on it 'My Main Thoughts in Performing Well' by Moe Norman," says Morris. There were about twenty-five one-liners that had been Moe's guiding principles throughout his career. You would think that they would have been all about the swing from such a legendary ball striker but take a look at some of them here. I would like for you to see that at least twelve of these have to do with perspective:

My Main Thoughts In Performing Well ---- "Moe" Norman

- Full extension "Back" and "Through".

- My club must never "Twist" or "Turn" in my swing.

- I play into my legs.

- I employ the least moving parts.

- I swing "Through" the ball, not "At" it.

- Swing the arms "Up" as the body "Turns Away".

- I let my swing "Balance" me.

- Every time I hit a shot, I feel like I am shaking hands with the flag stick.

- Try "Smarter" not "Harder".

- Don't say I "Gotta Do" anything in life. There is nothing you "Gotta Do". But I "Want To".

- Never think of the money, get the ball into the hole.

- What's the longest walk in golf? It's from the practice tee to the first tee. I don't care if it's 10 yards. It's the longest walk in golf. Winners take their swing with them. Losers don't.

- Don't let the game "Eat You", you "Eat The Game".

- You are what you "Think You Are".

- Winners see what they want, Losers see what they don't want.

- I let my clubs do the talking, not my "Mouth".

- Solid thinking "Good Golf", bad thinking "Bad Golf".

- Always be in a good frame of mind.

- I always play "Target Golf".

- Negative thinking hurts more than negative swinging.

- I always concentrate on playing one shot at a time.

- Believe 100% in my ability.

- I always believed in myself, not someone else.

- Stop being afraid of yourself.

- Stop being afraid of not doing well.

- Winners play golf automatically.

- Believing in your "Mental Image" will make you a Master.

- Golf isn't supposed to be work. It's to have fun.

- Imagination and visualization are my keys to success.

- Don't worry about when you're going to die, but how you will live.[2]

NOTES

NOTES

HOLE #17: DRIVE

FIND YOUR HUSTLE

Good things may come to those who wait, but only the things left by those who hustle.

—Unknown

At this point in the game you have to dig really deep. It has become very personal. You are a long way from the clubhouse. The gallery has dwindled. The energy you feed off has narrowed. You must rely on yourself. And whether you're on the course, at a career juncture, or starting a new project, you have to figure out how to maintain the momentum to get where you want to go. The drive to compete is solely on your shoulders, and you have to find your motivation. It's time to hustle.

First let's gather a basic understanding of what drive is. Drive is the emotional and active strength needed to confidently achieve one's purpose. Another definition is an innate, biologically determined urge to attain a goal or satisfy a need. It has five basic ingredients:

1. <u>Determination</u>: Purpose-driven achievement over something that is difficult.

2. <u>Reliability</u>: Confidence in one's abilities.

3.   Intensity: Great energy and commitment.

4.   Vigor: Active strength.

5.   Endurance: To hold out with unyielding resistance.

How well would you say you are currently displaying these characteristics? Rate yourself in each of these areas (1-10, 1 being weak and 10 being strong). Pause a moment to think about each one. What areas do you need to strengthen?

You will go through periods in life where you feel like you have lost all motivation. That is completely normal. Long lasting motivation can be hard to maintain. Lack of energy, personal issues, past disappointments . . . all of these things can affect your drive. Try a few simple strategies to get your momentum going again or when you just need to reignite your hustle.

Passion promotes enthusiasm and motivation. Passion is what moves people to action. This enduring concept has proven itself many times over the years. When I am at the stress point in my life and I need extra energy to continue, I pause and revisit my dream. Do you know what you are passionate about? If you are to add drive to your round you must often envision your desires. Not only is it important to see your goals from a first hole position, but also consider your destination.

You can use your past mistakes as motivation to fuel your fire to keep hustling. Determination and desire can help overcome any past disappointments. Don't stay there too long, but occasionally remembering why you are fighting is a good intensifier.

Set simple, specific, achievable goals that will excite and inspire you. Start with small goals, if necessary. There is nothing like simple accomplishment to get you motivated again. Eat the elephant one bite at a time.

Work extra hard during the "drive times" to avoid negative people, including yourself. It's like throwing water on a fire. There will certainly be people that you can't avoid but limit your contact. We all know a killjoy, so stay clear. And avoid self-criticism during the times you are trying to hustle. All negative talk is toxic and needs to be avoided at all costs.

Try watching or reading something inspiring. It's almost impossible not to get invigorated watching an underdog claw his way to victory. One word, *Miracle*.

Don't get stuck in the "blame game." You can generally find fault in someone else, a circumstance, or even society as to the reason why you currently are off your game. If you mentally lecture yourself on how life has abused you the natural reaction is to believe it. You become a product of your environment. Stop the mental nonsense and take control of your life. You are not the way you are because of someone else. Don't believe everything you think; take into captivity unproductive thinking. A champion quickly sees the blame game as faulty thinking and will take responsibility

One last strategy to get you back on track . . . take a mini vacation if you can to go reset your priorities and goals. And if you can't get away for an extended period, get out for a day or so. Sometimes stepping away and recharging is all it takes.

I recently read a quote from Les Brown, he said, "Go after your dreams as if your life depends on it, because it does." The characteristic of Drive is so admirable because it seems to take so much extra effort. Don't give up. The players that hustle the most are the ones that keep moving forward. You are not alone, fellow competitor. Your talents, dreams, and priorities go with you. And I for one am rooting for you.

TAKEAWAY PRINCIPLES ON DRIVE:

1.   Drive is the emotional and active strength needed to confidently achieve one's purpose.

2.   Drive has five basic ingredients:

a.   <u>Determination</u>: Purpose driven achievement over something that is difficult

b.   <u>Reliability</u>: Confidence in one's abilities

c.   <u>Intensity:</u> Great energy and commitment

d.   <u>Vigor</u>: Active strength

e.   <u>Endurance</u>: To hold out with unyielding resistance.

3.   Often you have to reignite your motivation and drive. That is perfectly natural.

SIMPLE STEPS:

*See detailed steps listed above.

RECOMMENDED READING:

- *Good to Great: Why Some Companies Make the Leap and Others Don't by Jim Collins*
- *How to Get Things Done: The Art of Stress-Free Productivity by David Allen*

WELL THAT'S INTERESTING . . .

While we are on the subject of drive and hustle . . . According to *The Guinness Book of World Records*, the fastest golf cart in the world is the Bandit by Plum Quick Motors, which achieved a speed of 191.12 km/h (118.76 mph) when driven by Robby Steen (USA) at the Darlington Dragway in Hartsville, South Carolina on October 31, 2014. This is the second time a cart from Plum Quick motors has taken the title for the "Fastest."[1]

NOTES

HOLE #18: VICTORY

FINISH WELL

As you walk down the fairway of life, you must smell the roses, for you only get to play one round.
—Ben Hogan

The final hole in the match is typically the hardest. Historically, it had its own name; they called it "The Finishing Hole." It is right here where most championships are decided. To get here requires obedience to all the principles found in this book. This is time to work the hardest. I'm afraid too many folks don't care to practically apply this truth, in fact they move in a divergent direction being held back by loss of momentum. To lose the power of the momentum you've created in life is most tragic. Friends, it's unhealthy and dangerous. In golf and life, you don't get what you wish for you get what you work for.

Why should you keep working? Perhaps you believe you've mastered the course. Therein lies the danger. Listen, no one ever truly masters the course. You wouldn't have to do much research on the subject to conclude that the course will master you if you don't stay focused. Dr. John C. Maxwell often warns those he teaches of the dangers of "Destination Disease." Destination disease is an illness that robs people of their influence. Do not assume you are finished because you just played the last hole. You must exchange that line of thinking with thoughts on how to continue to improve and positively influence others. The actual definition of influence is having an effect on the character, development, or behavior of someone or something. It's important to understand that you are influencing others every day, directly and indirectly, whether you want the responsibility or not, just through basic interaction. So, make it a goal to make every second count. That's true significance. To finish well requires a greater passion for influence than ever before. Significant people realize this and never stop influencing others. You have earned the right to speak, to teach, and to make an indelible impression. Eighteen is your greatest opportunity and your time to leave a legacy.

Now is the time to create a powerful attitude for achievement. Attitudes have a great impact on our lives. A good first shot on eighteen may keep you from mentally giving up on the game. Similarly, having a good attitude will keep you from giving up on the day. Be more focused than at any other point of the match. Follow through makes all the difference. Can you still hear a parent, coach, or the club pro chirping at you for a lack of follow through? How efficient is your swing without it? It's ugly! So is a life without follow through. So, when you feel like quitting, remember why you started. Visualize those you walk through life with as well as those who are just starting. Invest unselfishly in them and follow through.

Professional golfers that excel rarely quit. When a pro leaves the tour, he typically moves on to the Senior Tour. After time well spent many will make appearances, teach, mentor, and commentate. There is power in a life of longevity and commitment. It speaks volumes and carries credibility. Why do they keep going? They are working out of their purpose. Some people find it easier to be enthralled with their jobs than to deal with other difficult tasks or relationships. Too many folks spend way too much time desperately looking for satisfaction in their work. Most rarely find it, consequently they relegate themselves to an unsatisfactory work experience. When they are too burnt out to continue, they move on to something else. You see, they are searching for purpose in their work, which is a risky venture. Instead, why not work out of your purpose? Don't know your purpose yet? Then it's time to clarify. Continue to work on your priority and goal lists and define who you want to be. Once your purpose for life is clear, and you have established who you are, what you believe and how you will live, then go to work through that window of perspective. God has promised to meet our needs if we will work. A purpose-filled existence is where you will find satisfaction, contentment, and joy!

As you mature, you must clarify your purpose often. Generating a purpose statement for your life is critical. A purpose-driven life clearly maps a strategy for significant living. Why do you do what you do? When I was a boy growing up in South Florida, I remember with amazing fondness day trips to the beach with my parents. I couldn't wait to jump in, the bigger the waves the better. When we arrived, we would set out our beach blankets and umbrella with all our belongings and snacks. That place identified where I would enter the water. It gave me a location to return to; it was home for the day. I recall my parents' instructions like it was yesterday, "make sure you keep this blanket and umbrella in sight." They knew the waves and the current would pull me away from the safety of the recognizable "home base" we created. So, off I would go into the water. For a bit of time, I'd keep an eye on the umbrella. After a while, I would lose focus getting wholeheartedly caught up in the waves and dangerously forget the instructions I was given. It didn't take long for me to be pulled a great distance from the safety of "home base." Here is my advice: When you are being tossed around and pulled away, it can be easy to lose track of your purpose. So be diligent to protect it and keep it in mind always. This will keep you on a track of significance and positive influence. Don't lose sight of your umbrella.

Well, how are you going to finish? The amazing Dr. Seuss said, "Today I shall behave as if this is the day I will be remembered for." If there was ever a time to consider your legacy this is it. Remain strong, even if you are fatigued. Keep a smile on your face and keep swinging. I don't care how many putts it takes, be resolved. You can do this. This is where victory is found. Finish the round my friend and finish well.

TAKEAWAY PRINCIPLES ON VICTORY:

1.   In golf and life, you don't get what you wish for you get what you work for. And you are never truly finished working.

2.   You are never finished influencing. The actual definition of influence is having an effect on the character, development, or behavior of someone or something. It's important to understand that you are influencing others every day, directly and indirectly, whether you want the responsibility or not, just through basic interaction.

3.   As you mature, you must clarify your purpose often. Your game is not over.

SIMPLE STEPS:

1.   Make a list of who you influence in life. Coworkers, children, friends, etc. Now think about how you are influencing them.

2.   Write your victory speech. Include in it all those you want to thank and list out all you have achieved and all you hope to achieve in life. Think of it a bucket list of sorts.

RECOMMENDED READING:

- *Secretariat by William Nack (or you could watch the movie)*

WELL THAT INTERESTING . . .

What's a victory without a speech?

Nick Faldo, victory speech, The Open, Muirfield, 1992

Nick Faldo had always had a love-hate relationship with the media. So, after his win, his comments to the media were not so surprising, "I would just like to thank everybody for all the letters they've written in telling me that my putting's all wrong. I'd like to thank all the TV commentators for telling me how to practice and what to and not to do. And obviously without the press . . . What can I say about the press? I thank them from the bottom of my . . . the heart of my bottom."

Then he addressed the gallery, "The reasons why I say this—are you ready?—is because . . . I did it my way." And he started singing the classic Sinatra song.[1]

Jordan Spieth after his 2017 British Open Victory

In classic Spieth fashion, Jordan had an entire list of people to thank after he accepted the claret jug as the Champion Golfer of the Year. But most notably was his sincere thanks to his opponent Matt Kuchar, "Matt, I really enjoyed battling with you buddy," Spieth said on the eighteenth green at Royal Birkdale. "Obviously it could have went to either one of us, I got the good breaks today. What a great champion Matt Kuchar is, and what a class act.

I took about twenty minutes to play one of my shots today, and Matt took it in stride, smiled, and . . . there's not many people who would have done that. And it speaks to the man you are, and you set a great example for all of us."[2]

Sam Snead, victory speech, The Open, St Andrews, 1946

And sometimes less is more. After his win, Sam simply and snidely said, "It looks like there used to be a golf course here."

NOTES

NOTES

3

THE NINETEENTH HOLE: CELEBRATE

I would hope that understanding and reconciliation are not limited to the 19th hole alone.
—Gerald R. Ford

Everybody loves the nineteenth hole. Its exact location varies. But where it is located isn't as critical as what happens there. The nineteenth hole is simply a place set aside for celebration, relaxation, and reflection. The vast majority of my readers knew immediately where we were going with this. But there still may be a few readers new to the golf world thinking, "Kyle it was my understanding there were only eighteen holes." Technically, that's true. The nineteenth hole in golf is a slang term for a pub, bar, or restaurant usually on or near the golf course, often in the clubhouse where participants convene to.

What's the allure? Perhaps this scene displays comradery and time-worn tradition. This setting is attractive because one can finally experience a little mercy and consolation to ease the triple digit score. Or maybe it's time for a little smack talk, like the chiding of the foursome you just destroyed by one shot. Maybe it's as simple as a cool place to soothe the throat after five rigorous hours on the links. Why is this important? For the avid golfer the nineteenth is as much a part of the game as the previous eighteen holes. Whatever the case, this is the place you go to be a part of something more.

What's cool is everyone is welcome, and, once there, you are on equal ground. In this establishment, it's not just about your handicap or how good you look in your knickers. These are ordinary folks of all colors, shapes, sizes, and socio-economic status enjoying good times in an atmosphere where they are welcome to celebrate and commiserate, finding comfort and camaraderie.

Ok, I want to conclude with a nineteenth hole challenge. You ready? You need to celebrate! Seriously, even if you lose. Find something to celebrate. Crap is going to happen on and off of the golf course. That's life. But there is always something to celebrate. This goes back to perspective. You will be able to accept losses with more grace when you look for something worth celebrating, even if it's just the lesson. Your life will have so much more fulfillment when you celebrate all the little things that make it awesome every day. Don't just wait for a special occasion. I am sure you can come up with a few reasons to enjoy some good old fashion glass raisin' without much prompting. And at the end of the day, even if you lose, celebrate the fact that you were blessed to play the game in the first place.

NOTES

NOTES

ENDNOTES

Pre-Round

[1] "Surprising Stats." Simply Orderly. Accessed on April 2, 2019.
    http://simplyorderly.com/surprising-statistics/.

[2] "What are your golf superstitions?" PGA. Accessed on April 2, 2019.
    https://www.pga.com/news/golf-buzz/what-your-golf-superstitions.

"Superstitious Much?" Lost Golf Balls. Accessed April 2, 2019.
    https://blog.lostgolfballs.com/superstitious-much-15-golf-superstitions-
    of-famous-golfers-you-wont-believe.

"Do Pro Golfers Have Superstitions? Here are 5 That Do." Mel Sole. Accessed on
April 2, 2019.
    https://www.ritson-sole.com/blog/do-pro-golfers-have-superstitions-
here-are-5-that-do/.

Hole 1

[1] "From Calamity Jane to Phrankenwood: 18 most famous golf clubs in history."
Golf. Accessed
    on April 11, 2019.
    https://www.golf.com/equipment/photo/2017/02/13/18-most-famous-
    clubs-golf-history.

Hole 3

[1] "My Shot: Samuel L. Jackson." Guy Yocom. Golf Digest. Accessed April 13,
2019.
    https://www.golfdigest.com/story/myshot_gd0512.

Hole 4

[1] "Distracted." Dictionary.com. Accessed April 26, 2019.
    https://www.dictionary.com/browse/distracted.

[2] Organization. "Seven Days In Utopia Star Talks Tiger Woods And Golf
Aspirations." HuffPost.

December 07, 2017. Accessed April 21, 2019.
https://www.huffpost.com/entry/lucas-black-interview-golf-tiger-woods-seven-days_n_953497.

[3] "Q&A With Lee Trevino." Jaime Diaz. Golf Digest. Accessed on April 13, 2019.
https://www.golfdigest.com/story/lee_trevino.

Hole 5
[1] "Local Rules That Went Around the World." The Richmond Golf Club. Accessed on April 13, 2019.
https://www.therichmondgolfclub.com/wartime-rules/.

Hole 6
[1] "The 1969 Ryder Cup, the concession, and an unbelievable act of sportsmanship." Gwilym Brown.
Golf. Accessed on April, 13, 2019. https://www.golf.com/special-features/ryder-cup-1969-tie-may-be-kissing-your-sister.

Hole 7
[1] "How to Stop Negative Self-talk." Mayo Clinic. February 18, 2017. Accessed April 21, 2019.
https://www.mayoclinic.org/healthy-lifestyle/stress-management/in-depth/positive-thinking/art-20043950.

[2] Loren Eiseley, *The Star Thrower* (Mariner Books, 1979).

[3] "The Weird Japanese Hole-In-One Tradition." Knowledge Nuts. Accessed on April 13, 2019.
https://knowledgenuts.com/2013/09/09/the-weird-japanese-hole-in-one-tradition/.

Hole 8
[1] Turak, August. "Are You Coachable? The Five Steps to Coachability." Forbes. October 29, 2015.
Accessed April 21, 2019.
https://www.forbes.com/sites/augustturak/2011/09/30/are-you-coachable-the-five-steps-to-coachability/#911637524f66.

[2] "20 Facts about Golf." Deer Creek Golf Club. Accessed on April 15, 2019.
https://www.deercreekflorida.com/articles/20-surprising-facts-golf.

"Did You Know? 25 Golf Fun Facts." GolfNow. Accessed on April 15, 2019.
https://blog.golfnow.com/did-you-know-25-golf-fun-facts/.

"Interesting Golf History Trivia and Golf Facts." Gaelicmatters.com. Accessed on April 15, 2019.
https://www.gaelicmatters.com/golf-history-trivia.html.

Hole 9

[1] "Priority No. 1 for Phil Mickelson." Jaime Diaz. Golfworld. Accessed on April 15, 2019.
https://www.golfdigest.com/story/priority-no-1-for-phil-mickelson-family.

Hole 10

[1] "10 Pro Golfer Meltdowns." Ben Whitlock. Golf Monthly. Accessed on April 15, 2019.
https://www.golf-monthly.co.uk/features/the-game/10-pro-golfer-meltdowns-144927.

"The 20 Best Golf Tantrums of All Time." Luke Kerr-Dineen. USA Sports Today. Accessed on April, 19.
2019, https://ftw.usatoday.com/2016/07/the-20-best-golf-temper-tantrums-of-all-time.

"15 Most Notorious Golf Tantrums." Jeffrey Schmidt. Bleacher Report. Accessed on April 19, 2019.
https://bleacherreport.com/articles/837079-13-most-notorious-golfing-tantrums#slide0.

"High-Profile Golfing Tantrums (Angry Golfer Showcase)." Hole19 Golf Blog. Accessed on April 19,
2019. https://blog.hole19golf.com/high-profile-golfing-tantrums-angry-golfer-showcase/.

Hole 11

[1] "About Walking for Kids." Walking for Kids. Accessed on April 19, 2019.

http://walkingforkids.org/about/.

Hole 12
[1] "Lazy Days of Summer Golf." Golf Limerick Poems. Accessed on April 19,2019.
> http://reallifelimericks.com/2010/09/12/lazy-days-of-summer-golf/.

Hole 13
[1] Don Colbert, *The Seven Pillars of Health* (Realms Fiction, 2010).

[2] Ray Foley, *God Loves Golfers Best* (Sourcebooks, 2009).

"25+ Golf Puns You Will Never FORE Get." Thought Catalog. Accessed on April 19, 2019.
> https://thoughtcatalog.com/january-nelson/2018/08/golf-puns/.

"Bad Golfer - Golf Jokes and Course Humour - One Liners." BadGolfer.com. Accessed April 26, 2019.
> http://www.badgolfer.com/departments/jokes/one-liners1.htm.

"Golf One-Liners." Myrtle Beach Golf. June 26, 2009. Accessed April 26, 2019.
> https://www.myrtlebeachgolf.com/news/golf-one-liners/.

Hole 14
[1] Quoted from video footage from PGA Tour YouTube Channel. Accessed on April 19, 2019.
> https://www.youtube.com/pgatour

Hole 15
[1] "Your Guide to Ten of Golf's Unusual Rules." Today's Golfer. Accessed on April 20, 2019.
> https://www.todaysgolfer.co.uk/tips-and-tuition/rules-of-golf/your-guide-to-golfs-unusual-rules/

Hole 16
[1] TED. "Why You Should Define Your Fears Instead of Your Goals | Tim Ferriss." YouTube. July 14,
> 2017. Accessed April 20, 2019.
https://www.youtube.com/watch?v=5J6jAC6XxAI.

[2] "Moe's Swing Thoughts." Moe Norman Golf. August 16, 2017. Accessed April 22, 2019.

> http://moenormangolf.com/moe-norman/moes-swing-thoughts/.

Hole 17
[1] "Fastest Golf Cart." Guinness World Records. Accessed on April 20, 2019.

> http://www.guinnessworldrecords.com/world-records/fastest-golf-cart

Hole 18
[1] Adiaga2. "Nick Faldo 1992 Open Speech." YouTube. March 16, 2013. Accessed April 20, 2019.

> https://www.youtube.com/watch?v=2XJppZfXopw.

[2] "Jordan Spieth Has Kind Words for Matt Kuchar in Open Speech." The Official Website of Jordan

> Spieth. Accessed April 20, 2019.

http://www.jordanspiethgolf.com/article/jordan-spieth-has-
> kind-words-for-matt-kuchar-in-open-speech.

[3] Jenkins, Dan, and John Ueland. "British Open: The Best And Worst Of The Open." Golf Digest.

> Accessed April 20, 2019. https://www.golfdigest.com/story/british-open-jenkins-best-and-worst.

Made in the USA
Coppell, TX
30 July 2020